The
2026
Awakening

KIRK NELSON

Wright Publishing Company

Wright Publishing Company
1093 Sea Holly Court
Virginia Beach, Va. 23454

TABLE OF CONTENTS

To Maria

AUTHOR'S NOTE

According to America's greatest psychic, Edgar Cayce, there are prophecies built into the Great Pyramid that are correct as to the hour, day, year, place, country, nation, town, and individuals involved. This got me thinking, how can you build a monument to predict an hour, day, year, place, country, nation, town, and individuals involved 12,000 years into the future?

This question sent me on a quest to discover the answer. Is it real? I think so. I truly believe that I have cracked the code of prophecy in the Great Pyramid and the Sphinx, and I reveal it all in total in this book.

- Kirk Nelson

INTRODUCTION

Most people would say there is no way to know what will happen in the future, but there are those people with extraordinary abilities who can predict the future such as Jesus, Edgar Cayce, Nostradamus, etc... In this book we will examine their prophecies to get a clear vision of what will happen in the future, and how it will affect all of us.

First, we will examine the prophecies of Isaiah, Ezekiel, Jesus, and the other Bible prophets. They predict wars, earthquakes, famines, earth changes, and the mystical transformation of humankind to a higher realm of consciousness.

Second, we will look at the prophecies of America's greatest psychic, Edgar Cayce. Cayce accurately predicted the stock market crash of 1929 and the beginning of World War II. Cayce's prophecies about the Great Pyramid and the Sphinx are interesting to us because these monuments were placed as a guidepost of prophecy for our time. Beneath the Sphinx was placed a Hall of Records which will soon be opened to reveal our past and our future. I believe I have discovered where the entrance to this Hall of Records is and quite possibly when it will be opened. Also examined will be the prophecies contained in the Great Pyramid of Giza, where a French architect has discovered secret unopened chambers.

Third, we will examine the physical history of the human race, from primitive man to the new type of human body which will emerge in the future, the so-called Fifth Root Race, and how the sons of god used DNA introgression to create modern man.

Fourth, we will examine the history of UFOs and alien intervention on our planet from the Battle of Los Angeles to Roswell to Belgium to Phoenix. We will look at what the aliens have been up to the past 70 years, and what they will be doing in the future. Why were they so interested in American nuclear bases? Are they preparing to change human DNA to create a human hybrid? Are they aliens or angels?

Fifth, we will examine the incredible astrological aspects of 2024 through 2027, and how this could be the time period that all these prophecies will be fulfilled. We will look at specific dates during this time period to try to predict what will be happening during those years.

The truth is that we all have the ability to be prophets. The great psychic Edgar Cayce said that nothing important happens to us that isn't first previewed in a dream. This is because dreams are the easiest pathway for us to access the Universal Consciousness. Why? Because there are three layers of consciousness, the Conscious mind, the Subconscious, and the Superconscious. The Conscious mind is your awakened self, the one we are all used to. Your Subconscious becomes active when you sleep. Your Superconscious is the part of all of us that is connected to the Universal Consciousness or God. When you sleep, your Subconscious becomes your Conscious giving you much closer access to your Superconscious. Here's an example...
One day I dreamed that my friend Tom came to visit me, and he was

wearing a yellow shirt. I woke up thinking, "That was weird. Why would I dream that?" I had not seen Tom in years and had no idea that he would be coming to visit. Well, that night Tom walked into my house wearing a canary yellow shirt. I nearly fell down. I became a believer in the prophetic power of dreams right then.

There are many examples of prophetic dreams in the Bible. Jacob, Joseph, and Daniel in the Old Testament all had prophetic dreams. In the New Testament Joseph became concerned when Mary became pregnant before their marriage, but an angel appeared to him in a dream, saying, "Joseph, do not fear to take Mary as your wife, for that which is conceived in her is from the Holy Spirit." Then after Jesus was born, Joseph was warned in a dream to take his family to Egypt, so Herod could not kill Jesus. Joseph did so. When Herod finally died, Joseph had a dream telling him it was safe to return. So, it is very important to listen to your dreams, my friends, because they can be prophetic.

Which brings me to how I came to write this book. I have been a student of prophecy for over 40 years. I started in the 1960's reading Jeanne Dixon's book, A Gift of Prophecy, Hal Lindsey's book, The Late Great Planet Earth, and Jess Stern's book, The Sleeping Prophet. I then became an astrologer and spent the next thirty years studying the effects of planetary influences on people and world events. I wrote several books and lectured around the country for years, but I got away from it and got into real estate the last 16 years or so. Then I had a dream.

I dreamed that I was looking at a wall covered with vines and moss that looked neglected. I thought, "This is ridiculous! Someone should clean this up!" So I looked down and saw a magic broom at my feet. I took the broom and touched the wall, and everywhere I touched the moss and vines fell away, and there was a left a stainless steel Hall of Fame. I woke up and thought, "Oh, I have to get back involved with metaphysics."

So after discussing the possibilities with my literary agent, I decided to write a book that encompasses my 40 year study of prophecy.

Lest we take any predictions too seriously, we should remember the case of William Miller, whose story is retold in the following quote from the book, *Did Jesus Write This Book?* by Charles Francis Potter:

"**The nineteenth and twentieth centuries have also produced prophecies of the 'end of days.' The last century brought the once famed William Miller, an American who founded a sect named after himself. Like his predecessors of the A.D. 999 hoax, Miller calculated his end-all date from biblical mathematics, particularly those obscure calculations in Daniel (8:14). Christ will return on March 21, 1843, or March 21, 1844, Miller told his followers, who prepared their ascension robes in readiness for their translation into heaven. Twice the faithful gathered for the glorious meeting, and twice nothing happened. 'The World is reeling to and fro like a drunkard,' the leader assured the Millerites, but all that appeared in the sky were ominous rings around the sun, and the awesome tail of the great comet of 1843, measuring 108,000,000 miles in length.**

"**Sorrowfully, after this double fiasco, the only world to end was Miller's. Thousands of followers deserted him. A broken man, he died alone in his Vermont home, discredited and beaten by his own honest delusion.**"

Unlike the Millerites, we should not don our ascension robes and prepare for the end. But there are certain signs that will tell us when these great changes are close. These signs are, I believe, clearly discernible and will become apparent to all of us as the time draws near.

THE BIBLE PROPHETS

Imagine the scene two thousand years ago....

The disciples are sitting on Mount Olives overlooking the city of Jerusalem waiting for Jesus to tell them about the future....

Matthew 24:3-30

And as he sat on Mount Olives, the disciples came to him privately saying, Tell us, when shall these things be? And what shall be the sign of your coming and the end of the age?

And Jesus answered them and said to them, Take heed that no man deceive you.

For many shall come in my name, saying, I am Christ; and shall deceive many.

And you shall hear of wars and rumors of wars; See that you are not troubled for all these things must come to pass, but the end is not yet.

For nation shall rise against nation, and kingdom against kingdom; and there shall be famines, and pestilences, and earthquakes, in various places.

All these things are the beginning of sorrows.

Then shall they deliver you up to be afflicted and shall kill you; and you shall be hated of all nations for my name's sake.

And then shall many be offended and shall betray one another.

And many false prophets shall rise and shall deceive many.

And because iniquity shall abound, the love of many shall grow cold.

But he that shall endure to the end, the same shall be saved.

And this gospel of the kingdom shall be preached in all the world for a witness to all nations; and then shall the end come.

When you, therefore, shall see the abomination of desolation, spoken of by Daniel the prophet, stand in the holy place (whoever reads let him understand).

Then let them who are in Judea flee into the mountains;

Let him who is on the housetop not come down to take anything out of his house;

Neither let him who is in the field return back to take his clothes.

And woe to those who are with child, and to those who nurse children in those days!

But pray that your flight be not in the winter, neither on the sabbath day;

For then shall be great tribulation, such as was not since the beginning of the world to this time, no, nor ever shall be.

And except those days should be shortened, there should no flesh be saved; but for the elect's sake those days shall be shortened.

Immediately after the tribulation of those days shall the sun be darkened and the moon shall not give its light, and the stars shall fall from heaven, and the powers of the heavens shall be shaken.

And then shall appear the sign of the Son of man in heaven; and then shall all the tribes of the earth mourn, and they shall see the Son of man coming in the clouds of heaven with power and great glory.

Jesus outlines to the disciples events which will happen in the future. They are…

- **The Abomination of Desolation**
- **The Great Tribulation**
- **The Darkening of the Sun and the Moon**
- **The Return of Jesus**

The Abomination of Desolation

What is an abomination of desolation? It is a term that refers to the desecration of the Jewish temple in Jerusalem. This desecration occurs when a sinful object is brought into the sacred part of the temple, where only the priests are allowed to enter. An example would be if a pig were offered on the holy altar, or if an altar to a pagan god were built in the holy place. A Syrian king, Antiochus Epiphanes, defiled the temple in just such a manner in 165 B.C. In order for another abomination of desolation to occur, the Jews must build a new temple. The last Jewish temple in Jerusalem was destroyed in 70 A.D. by the invading Romans. However, since the Israelis recaptured Jerusalem in the 1967 war, they have begun excavating the ancient temple site. This has created a problem because the Moslem holy place, the Dome of the Rock, is built on the site of the old Jewish temple. This makes the Temple Mount sacred to both the Moslems and the Jews, and both claim it as their own. We can see how important the temple site is to the Jews from this description of the Israelis' capture of the Temple Mount in 1967 after 2,000 years of dispersement:

"**The Israeli paratroop commander Mordechae Gur from atop Mount Olives ordered the final assault on the Temple Mount, 'For two thousand years our people have prayed for this moment. Let us go forward.'**

Colonel Gur could not wait. He raced his halftrack down the mountain at top speed, hurling past the burned-out hulks of tanks and the sprawling bodies of slain paratroopers, then dodged by a flaming truck partly blocking St. Stephen's Gate and burst right into the Old City.

White flags were beginning to appear on all sides. While his paratroopers reared in behind him, the colonel turned left, crashed through another gate and then sent back his message to GHQ: 'The Temple Mount is ours. Repeat: The Temple Mount is ours.' And despite the crackle of continued sniper fire, the first paratroopers rushed to the Western Wall, touched and kissed the sacred stones, then burst into tears at their triumph."*

***Time* magazine, April 12, 1982, p. 30, New York, N.Y., "City of Protest and Prayer," Otto Friedrich.**

The Western Wall is a holy place to the Jews because it is the outside wall of the temple that was destroyed in 70 A.D. Recently they have begun to excavate the area near it and the steps that led to the temple on the other side of the mount along the Southern Wall. Over the years layer after layer of debris has built up on the site of the old temple, and it will take some time to uncover it.

In the Book of Exodus in the Old Testament are instructions for the construction of the temple and also instructions on how to perform the temple worship. Part of this worship involves the sacrificing of animals. This sacrifice is so important to the Jews that when they recaptured the Temple Mount in 1967, they wanted to begin again this daily ritual. The reason they did not is that they did not know the location of the old altar, since it is buried beneath the site of the Dome of the Rock.

The exact location of the temple's altar is important because according to Jewish law the sacrifice can only take place on the exact spot of the original altar. For many years it has been theorized that the altar was located under the Moslem holy place, the Dome of the Rock, from where, according to legend, Mohammed ascended into heaven.

Jesus tells us that the abomination of desolation will "stand in the holy place." This is a very specific reference to part of the temple. The inner sanctuary of the temple has two parts: the holy place and the holy of holies. Only the priests in their daily ritual are allowed to enter the holy place. It is the spot where they burn incense and light the lampstand. The holy of holies is the most sacred part of the temple, which only the high priest is allowed to enter once a year on the Day of Atonement. On that day, the high priest enters the holy of holies and sprinkles the blood of the sacrifice to make atonement for the sins of the Jewish people. So the abomination of desolation will not take place in the innermost sanctuary but in the holy place just outside.

It is possible, however, that the abomination of desolation could occur without the temple being rebuilt. The term could refer to the desecration of the Temple Mount itself rather than a rebuilt temple. For this reason events involving the Temple Mount should be watched closely in the future.

The Great Tribulation

After the abomination of desolation Jesus tells us that there will be a great tribulation, a time of trouble more tumultuous than any time that ever has been or will be on the earth. The events in this time period may involve war in the Middle East and earth changes. There will not be a full-scale nuclear war, however. In Matthew 24 Jesus says that if this time were not cut short, then no one would be saved. So, clearly, any conflicts during this time will end before they lead to all-out nuclear war. Jesus' reference to total destruction shows that Jesus foresaw the invention of nuclear weapons and the ultimate question that we are now faced with, "Do we live in peace or do we destroy ourselves?"

The Darkening of the Sun and the Moon

The above-mentioned verses from Matthew are quotes from Jesus, just after He has told the disciples about the abomination of desolation and the tribulation. He tells them that immediately after the tribulation, the sun and the moon will be darkened. This reference to the darkening of the sun and the moon is predicted in at least half a dozen places in the Bible: in Isaiah, Joel, Zachariah, Luke, and Revelation. The fact that it is mentioned so many times shows that it is a very important omen of change.

Obviously, for the sun to be darkened would require some catastrophic event. One that has been suggested is the eruption of many of the earth's 200 volcanoes within a very short length of time. This would throw so much dust and volcanic ash into the air that it would cause darkness at noon-day. This happened in some cities in Washington State when Mount St. Helens erupted.

The Revelation states that the moon will be as red as blood. Dust particles in the air diffract light, and this can cause the moon to appear red. Volcanic ash can also cause this effect. When a volcano on the island of Krakatoa exploded in the late 1800s, it set off a rash of sunset portraits in England because the particles released into the air created beautiful sunsets all over the world. Revelation states that the heavens will disappear like "a scroll when it is rolled together." This implies some type of smoke or dust cloud. When clouds roll in, they make the sky disappear in the same way a scroll disappears when it is rolled together.

Other possible causes for the darkening of the sun and moon are solar and lunar eclipses. These are the only times when we are used to the sun being darkened by the moon, and the moon being made red by being put in the earth's shadow. If the earth were to shift on its axis, then we would have solar and lunar eclipses that were not expected.

The possibility of a pole shift seems to be implied in Matthew 24 when it says that the "powers of the heavens will be shaken." What are the powers of heaven? In physics they are gravitation, rotation, and inertia. A pole shift would certainly shake these powers. Also Revelation says that "every mountain and island [will be] moved out of their places," an occurrence that would require a shift of the whole earth, causing volcanic eruptions and earthquakes. Interestingly enough, earthquakes can also throw up dust and make the sky darken. This occurred in the United States during the great Missouri quake of 1811.

Scientists tell us that we are currently in the middle of a magnetic pole reversal. This is when the earth's north and south magnetic poles reverse positions. When this happens, the strength of the earth's magnetic field drops to zero, and the earth is no longer protected from deadly cosmic radiation. Scientists originally thought that this reversal was 1,500 years away, but recently they discovered that the earth's magnetic field is decaying at a rate 50 times faster than they thought. A magnetic field reversal could be the cause of the darkening of the sun and the moon, by some mechanism that we have never seen before.

After these earth changes occur, Jesus tells us that his sign will appear in heaven. His sign may be a cross or a star, like the star of Bethlehem. If it is the sign of the cross, it might be formed by planetary conjunctions or some other celestial phenomena. What the sign will be we cannot be certain, but the cross and the star of Bethlehem are Jesus' symbols.

The darkening of the sun and moon are the most important signs to look for as the end of the age. As stated earlier, in terms of numbers this particular omen is mentioned in the Bible more than any other as a foreshadowing of Jesus' return—over a half dozen times in the Old and New Testaments. It is also mention in the Koran and the Jewish holy books, so three of the world's major religions recognize this as an omen of prophecy.

Here is the passage of Daniel that Jesus refers to in Matthew 24:

Daniel 11:40-45

And at the time of the end shall the King of the South push at him; and the King of the North shall come against him like a whirlwind, with chariots, and with horsemen, and with many ships; and he shall enter into the countries, and shall overflow and pass through.

He shall enter also into the glorious land, and many countries shall be overthrown, but these shall escape out of his hand, even Edom, and Moab, and the chief of the Children of Ammon.

He shall stretch forth his hand also upon the countries, and the land of Egypt shall not escape.

But he shall have power over the treasures of gold and of silver, and over all the precious things of Egypt; and the Libyans and the Ethiopians shall be at his steps.

But tidings out of the east and out of the north shall trouble him; therefore, he shall go forth with great fury to destroy, and utterly to sweep away many.

And he shall plant the tabernacles of his palace between the seas in the glorious holy mountain; yet he shall come to his end, and none shall help him.

Daniel 12:1

And at that time shall Michael stand up, the great prince who stands for the children of your people and there shall be a time of trouble, such as never was since there was a nation even to that same time; and at that time your people shall be delivered, every one that shall be found written in the book.

This passage deals with an invasion of the Middle East by a future king. He will enter the glorious land (Israel) and pass through into Egypt. We know that these verses refer to the time of the end because the passage begins with the phrase "at the time of the end." Plus, the events described in this section of Daniel have never been fulfilled.

This next point is very, very important. Verse 1 of Daniel 12 shows us that the invasion will occur at the beginning of the tribulation because the wording of this verse is identical to Jesus' description of the tribulation in Matthew 24. Jesus was familiar with the book of Daniel and realized that He was quoting from Daniel in describing the events preceding His return. He and Daniel both say that the tribulation will be a time of trouble such as never seen before. Verse 11:45 states that the invader will "plant the tabernacles of his palace between the seas in the glorious holy mountain." It is possible that the mountain referred to is not only the land of Israel but the Temple Mount itself in Jerusalem. So after the invasion the invader will set up his headquarters in Israel, possibly in Jerusalem.

The military aspects of this war in the Middle East provide us with clues as to who the invader will be. Daniel says that the Libyans and the Ethiopians "shall be at his steps." This means they will be servants of the invader or, as it is called in war, allies. This is not surprising, since both Libya and Ethiopia are at present bitter enemies of Israel. Daniel states that the lands of Edom and Moab and Ammon will escape invasion. These names were used in biblical times to describe what is now the country of Jordan. This fits, since Jordan is a traditional enemy of Israel.

One of the most interesting aspects in all this is that both Israel and Egypt will be invaded and possibly allied together against the invader.

After Egypt and Israel are subdued, the invading king will be disturbed by tidings out of the North and East and shall go forth to kill many people. But as Daniel tells us, he will come to his end, and no one will help him. Whether he will be destroyed by men or by an act of God is not made clear, but he will ultimately be destroyed.

The Michael written of in Daniel 12 is Michael the Archangel. He is the Lord of the Way. He will deliver the souls of all that are written in the Book of Life. Those who have followed the true spirit of the Christ Consciousness, whatever their religion, will be delivered. Before this, however, a great military power must arise and defeat Israel and Egypt in a war, and this will take a very strong army indeed.

Ezekiel 38 10-23

Therefore, son of man, prophesy and say to Gog, Thus says the Lord; In that day when my people of Israel live safely, shalt you not know it? And you shalt come from your place out of the north, you, and many people with you, all of them riding upon horses, a great company, and a mighty army: And you shall come up against my people of Israel, as a cloud to cover the land; it shall be in the latter days, and I will bring you against my land, that the heathen may know me, when I shall be sanctified in you, O Gog, before their eyes.

Thus said the Lord; Are you he of whom I have spoken in old time by my servants the prophets of Israel, which prophesied in those days many years that I would bring you against them? And it shall come to pass at the same time when Gog shall come against the land of Israel, said the Lord, that my fury shall come up in my face. For in my jealousy and in the fire of my wrath have I spoken, Surely in that day there shall be a great shaking in the land of Israel; So that the fishes of the sea, and the fowls of the heaven, and the beasts of the field, and all creeping things that creep upon the earth, and all the men that are upon the face of the earth, shall shake at my presence, and the mountains shall be thrown down, and the steep places shall fall, and every wall shall fall to

the ground. And I will call for a sword against him throughout all my mountains, said the Lord: every man's sword shall be against his brother. And I will plead against him with pestilence and with blood; and I will rain upon him, and upon his bands, and upon the many people that are with him, an overflowing rain, and great hailstones, fire, and brimstone. Thus will I magnify myself, and sanctify myself; and I will be known in the eyes of many nations, and they shall know that I am the Lord.

This passage of Ezekiel is another description of this future invasion of Israel by what Ezekiel calls Gog and Magog. Ezekiel says they will come like a "cloud upon the land." George Lamsa, who translated this passage from the original Aramaic, translates Gog and Magog as China and Mongolia. China is a growing economic and military power with the largest army in the world, and they could easily access the Middle East by land.

Another possibility for this invader would be Russia. Russia has invaded the countries of Georgia and Ukraine recently and has a very powerful military and a very nationalistic leader in Vladimir Putin.

According to Ezekiel the invader will ultimately be destroyed by fire and brimstone. Several possibilities that might fit this description are nuclear weapons, earth changes, or cosmic rays from a magnetic field reversal.

Ezekiel's Spaceship

Many people believe that the following passage of Ezekiel describes an alien spaceship. NASA scientist Josef F. Blumrich wrote a book about this passage of Ezekiel in which he suggests that a prototype craft based on Ezekiel's description could be built.

Ezekiel 1: 15-24

Now as I saw the living creatures, behold one wheel upon the earth by the living creatures, with his four faces. The appearance of the wheels and their work was like the color of a beryl: and they four had one likeness: and their appearance and their work was as it were a wheel in the middle of a wheel. When they went, they went upon their four sides: and they turned not when they went. As for their rings, they were so high that they were dreadful; and their rings were full of eyes round about them four. And when the living creatures went, the wheels went by them: and when the living creatures were lifted up from the earth, the wheels were lifted up. Whithersoever the spirit was to go, they went, thither was their spirit to go; and the wheels were lifted up over against them: for the spirit of the living creature was in the wheels. When those went, these went; and when those stood, these stood; and when those were lifted up from the earth, the wheels were lifted up over against them: for the spirit of the living creature was in the wheels.

And the likeness of the firmament upon the heads of the living creature was as the color of the terrible crystal, stretched forth over their heads above. And under the firmament were their wings straight, the one toward the other: every one had two, which covered on this side, and every one had two, which covered on that side, their bodies. And when they went, I heard the noise of their wings, like the noise of great waters, as the voice of the Almighty, the voice of speech, as the noise of an host: when they stood, they let down their wings.

Ezekiel's spaceship is only one of several historical accounts of UFO visitations. Few people know that Columbus saw UFOs on the way to the New World, and the Apollo 11 astronauts saw UFOs on the way to the moon.

EDGAR CAYCE'S PROPHECIES

Edgar Cayce was the greatest psychic in American history. He lived from 1877-1945 and gave over 14,000 readings, the majority of which were recorded and are still preserved. Cayce's expertise was diagnosing illness, and most of his readings were devoted to healing the sick.

Cayce would lie on his couch, go into trance, and after being given only the name and address of the sick person, would give an accurate diagnosis including the appropriate remedies. Cayce's abilities were so profound that his fame put him on the front page of the magazine section of the *New York Times* on October 9, 1910.

The followers of Edgar Cayce formed an organization called the Association for Research and Enlightenment, Inc., to study and research his psychic readings. The A.R.E., with headquarters in Virginia Beach, still exists today and boasts a membership of over 30,000. The headquarters contains a large library, bookstore, and records of Cayce's 14,000 readings. Edgar Cayce gave approximately 2,000 life readings. These involve reincarnation, personal and business problems, and sometimes prophecy. The readings in which Cayce gave prophetic information are the ones that are of interest to us.

In one of these readings Cayce accurately predicted a real estate boom for Virginia Beach, including the year in which it would end. Years before it happened, he stated in a reading that Norfolk would be the number one seaport on the east coast surpassing New York. This is now the case.

Another of Cayce's predictions was that the lost continent of Atlantis would be discovered off the coast of the Caribbean island of Bimini in 1968 or 1969. This prophecy was fulfilled by a group of divers who discovered large rectangular stones beneath the ocean just off Bimini's shore. Much of the later discoveries involving these stones are chronicled in Dr. David Zink's book, *Stones of Atlantis.*

Dr. Zink mapped and explored the ruins and brought forth evidence that these rock formations were man-made. Amazing as it is, Cayce predicted the location and the year that the "stones of Atlantis" would be discovered.

Another prediction Cayce made was that a crystal power source would be discovered by scientists in 1958. The main theoretical papers that led to the invention of the laser (which uses a ruby crystal to amplify light) were put forward in 1958. Once again, Cayce was correct as to the year and the event.

The above-mentioned fulfilled prophecies show that Edgar Cayce had the ability to predict the future. This is not to say, however, that Cayce's predictive powers were infallible. He forecast earth changes for the state of Alabama in the 1930s that did not come about. The "sleeping prophet" always insisted that humans had free will and by acting in accordance with God's laws could change the future. Frequently, he stated that a group of people praying together could save a city, a state, or a region. This seems to be what happened when Cayce's predictions did not come true.

The Cayce readings contain several references which apply to our study of the invader of the Middle East mentioned in the bible, and here is the first of these:

As is indicated in that period where entrance is shown to be in that land that was set apart, as that promised to that peculiar peoples, as were rejected—as is shown in that portion when there is the turning back from the raising up of Xerxes as the deliverer from an unknown tongue or land, and again is there seen that this occurs in the entrance of the Messiah in this period— 5748-5

Cayce in the first part of this reading is speaking of the first entrance of Jesus to the earth "in that period," namely the first century A.D. The entrance point was Bethlehem, part of the Promised Land or, as Cayce puts it, "that promised to that peculiar peoples." The phrase "as were rejected" refers to the rejection of the Jews by God when they were carried into Babylonian captivity. The next phrase is the key point. Cayce states that there was a "turning back from the raising up of Xerxes as the deliverer" and that this would occur again during the entrance of the Messiah. The "Messiah" Cayce is referring to is Jesus, so this is one of the readings in which Cayce predicts that Jesus will return.

In the previous reading Cayce referred to a Xerxes involved with the entrance of the Messiah and this reference to Xerxes requires some historical background to explain. Xerxes was a very powerful Persian king who assembled an enormous army, conquered Greece, and burned Athens to the ground. His army is considered to be the largest army ever assembled in ancient times. Xerxes' rule stretched from Greece to India and included Arabia, the Holy Land, Persia, and Egypt. He was described as "lecherous and cruel" and was well known as a desecrator of temples! Sounds very much like the invader, doesn't it?

Wherever Xerxes went, he burned down and destroyed temples established to worship local deities. Preceding Persian kings had attempted to appease their subject people by respecting local gods, but Xerxes did just the opposite. He wrecked temples in Egypt, Babylon, and Greece. In Babylon, he went into the temple of Zeus, stole a gold statue of the ancient god, and killed a priest who attempted to stop him.

All of this would be enough to show us that Cayce was alluding to the invader in this reading, but when you examine the relationship between the Persian kings and the Jews, the parallels become amazing. The four most important Persian kings mentioned in the Bible were:

Cyrus the Great (r. 550-530 B.C.) Darius (r. 521-486 B.C.)
Xerxes (r. 486-465 B.C.) Artaxerxes (b. 465-425 B.C.)

Cyrus the Great conquered the Babylonians and permitted the Jews to return to the Holy Land and rebuild the temple. Artaxerxes, the son of Xerxes, allowed the Jewish leader Nehemiah to return to Jerusalem and rebuild the walls of the city. The story of this is in the biblical Books of Ezra and Nehemiah. As you can see, the Persian kings were deeply involved in the return of the Jews to the Holy Land, the reestablishment of the temple worship, and the rebuilding of the walls of Jerusalem.

Considering that the invader may be instrumental in dealings to allow the Jews to keep Jerusalem and reestablish temple worship, the similarity between the invader and the ancient Persian kings is striking.

But what about Xerxes? After Darius died, there was some debate as to who would be the new king. Xerxes was chosen because he was the oldest son of Darius and because he had a kingly look and manner. The Book of Esther in the Old Testament records the history of Xerxes and the Jews. In the Old Testament Xerxes is known by his Hebrew name, Ahasuerus. Cayce describes him in the following paragraph:

. . . Ahasuerus [Xerxes] came to the throne in the early twenties, and was not an uncouth man; yet— with the ease of the conditions and surroundings —being lauded by the princes of the various charges over which the counselors came—he became rather what would be termed in the present as a dissipated man. He was one, though, fair in the GENERAL outlook but with a very decided Roman nose (as would be called in the present), with hazel eyes, with fair hair; the weight being a hundred and seventy-six pounds (as would be termed in the present: then called duets [?]). This was his general mien. 1096-3

Xerxes was a tall, kingly looking man when he assumed the throne, but because of the ease of conditions he gradually eroded into what Cayce called a "dissipated man." It would seem that this was his condition at the time the Book of Esther was written, for the first part of Esther describes Xerxes as feasting and drinking for seven days in his palace. During this drinking bout he ordered his beautiful queen, Vashti, to come and dance for the entertainment of his guests, but she refused. This made Xerxes decide to dethrone her and choose a new queen. He felt that Vashti's refusal would cause women throughout his kingdom to refuse the commands of their husbands.

So the search went out for a new queen, one of great beauty to be chosen. Ultimately, Esther, a Jew, was chosen. However, Xerxes did not know that she was a Jew, because she had been told by Mordecai, her kinsman, not to reveal this to the king. During Esther's reign as queen, Haman, one of the king's advisors, convinced the king that the Jews were an evil people and that they should be destroyed. Xerxes issued the following proclamation:

Esther 3:13

And the letters were sent by posts into all the King's provinces, to destroy, to kill, and cause to perish, all Jews, both young and old, little children and women, in one day even upon the thirteenth day of the twelfth month, which is the month Adar, and to take the property of them for spoil.

So after being friendly with the Jews and letting them work on the rebuilding of the temple begun under Cyrus, Xerxes changed his mind and ordered all the Jews in his kingdom killed. This is exactly the scenario that interpreters of Bible prophecy have predicted for the end times: a powerful leader will make a deal with the Jews, allow them to reestablish temple worship, and then turn against them.

As students of the Bible know, Xerxes' mind was eventually changed by his Queen Esther, and he did not kill all the Jews. But Cayce was drawing a parallel here of a leader who was a friend to the Jews at first and later changed his mind. One thing to remember is that Cayce was an avid student of the Bible, having read it cover to cover once for every year of his life. Therefore, he was familiar with the story of Xerxes in the Book of Esther and with the fact that a future "Xerxes" was prophesied in the Bible.

Cayce on Daniel's invader

On September 25, 1939 (twenty-four days after the beginning of World War II), Edgar Cayce was asked the following question:

Q. For what real purpose is the present war?

A. Read in Daniel, the last two chapters, and see; also the 31st of Deuteronomy—and we will see. 257-211

This reading was given for a Jewish man who wanted to know the real purpose of World War II. Cayce repeatedly stated in other readings that the reason for Hitler's rise to power in Germany was so that the Jews would return to their own land, Palestine. Chapter 31 of Deuteronomy, which Cayce recommended to this man, has to do with the return of the Jews to their own land. In this chapter of Deuteronomy Moses lectures the Jews just before they are to cross the Jordan River into Palestine.

What Cayce is saying in the above reading is that World War II was the catalyst for the Jews' return to their own land and the fulfillment of the prophecies of the last two chapters of Daniel. At the end of World War II, part of the settlement agreement stated that because of the extermination camps and the persecution of the Jews by the Germans, the Jews needed a homeland. Palestine was selected and ultimately given up by the British to provide a homeland for the Jews.

The last two chapters in Daniel are Daniel 11 and 12. These chapters predict an invasion of the Middle East prior to Jesus' return.

There is also evidence in the following Cayce reading for a Chinese invasion:

If there is not the acceptance in America of the closer brotherhood of man, the love of the neighbor as self, civilization must

---

wend its way westward—and again must Mongolia, must a hated people, be raised. 3976-15

A concept that is constantly brought up in the Cayce readings is that the leadership of civilization is continuously moving westward. First came the Roman Empire, then the British Empire, and today we have the American "Empire," each farther west than the preceding.

In the above reading Cayce tells us that if the United States does not live up to its obligations with respect to the love of its neighbors and all humankind, then civilization will move west and the Mongols will again sweep the world. The modern-day Mongol empire is, of course, China.

Since this reading says that a hated people of Mongolia must again be raised, it would be good for us to look back at the last time Mongolia was the center of an empire.

In the early thirteenth century, a Mongol tribal chieftain named Temuchin began conquering a large area of Mongolia. As his power grew, he organized a huge, swiftly moving, well-disciplined army and assumed the name Genghis Khan or "Very Mighty King." Genghis expanded his empire to include China and large sections of Asia. Khan's warriors were particularly noted for their savagery. Genghis died in 1227, and his successors, Ogodei Khan and Kublai Khan, increased the size of the empire by further conquest and made Beijing its capital city. By the late thirteenth century, the Mongol Empire stretched from the Pacific Ocean to the Black Sea and included the area of what is now Afghanistan, Pakistan, Iran, Iraq, Central Russia, Hungary, and Poland. The invasion route taken by the Mongols in conquering these countries is the same one that

28

China would have to take to invade the Middle East today. All in all, Cayce drew an excellent parallel for us.

Earth Changes

Now let us turn to the Cayce readings and see what they have to say about the coming earth changes.

As to the material changes that are to be as an omen, as a sign to those that this is shortly to come to pass—as has been given of old, the sun will be darkened and the earth shall be broken up in divers places—and THEN shall be PROCLAIMED— through the spiritual interception in the hearts and minds and souls of those that have sought His way—that HIS star has appeared, and will point the way for those that enter into the holy of holies in themselves. For, God the Father, God the Teacher, God the director, in the minds and hearts of men, must ever be IN those that come to know Him as first and foremost in the seeking of those souls; for He is first the GOD to the individual and as He is exemplified, as He is manifested in the heart and in manifested before men . . .

As to the changes physical again: The earth will be broken up in the western portion of America. The greater portion of Japan must go into the sea. The upper portion of Europe will be changed as in the twinkling of an eye. Land will appear off the east coast of America. There will be the upheavals in the Arctic and in the Antarctic that will make for the eruption of volcanoes in the Torrid areas, and there will be shifting then of the poles—so that where there has been those of a frigid or the semitropical will become the more tropical, and moss and fern will grow. And these will begin in those periods in '58 to '98, when these will be proclaimed as the periods when His light will be seen again in the clouds. As to times, as to seasons, as to places, ALONE is it given

to those who have named the name—and who bear the mark of those of His calling and His election in their bodies. To them it shall be given. 3976-15

In this reading Cayce mentions the darkening of the sun which is written about so often in the bible. Also mentioned along with this is the "breaking up" of the earth by earthquakes, again, just as the bible says. In addition, upheavals in the Arctic will cause volcanoes elsewhere to erupt. All of these changes will be in connection with a pole shift.

Volcanic eruptions have caused weather changes in the past. In 1815 the Mount Tambora volcano in Indonesia erupted and released so much dust into the atmosphere that the sun's rays were reflected, creating a very cool a summer" because temperatures were still winter like in the Northeast well into June. In 1982 the eruption of the Mexican volcano, El Chichon, caused a dust cloud that extended all the way around the world. Scientists immediately feared that the cloud would cool off the earth's weather, especially since the cloud was situated at the equator, where the Earth gets most of its heat. Any major change in the Earth's weather could cause crop failure and lead to famine. It has been discovered that the Earth's polar axis shifts a few feet every year. This shift was named the "Chandler wobble." It could be that this slight wobble in the axis could work its way into a major shift much in the same way that a slight wobble in a spinning top can accelerate it and cause it to fall over after a few turns.

According to Cayce, the last pole shift occurred 50,000 years ago. This information dovetails with evidence that has been found. In Siberia in the early 1900s, woolly mammoths were discovered frozen solid with summer food in their stomachs. Their bodies were so perfectly preserved that experts estimate only a quick freeze could have done the trick. Only a pole shift could have changed the weather so radically and so quickly that their bodies were frozen with no hint of decomposition. The radiocarbon dating of these mammoths put their deaths at between 44,000 and 48,000 B.C., the time period when Cayce says the last pole shift occurred. These mammoths were used by Immanuel Velikovsky in his book, *Worlds in Collision,* as an example of past catastrophic earth changes.

In the latter part of the previous reading, Cayce states that changes will occur in America, Japan, and Europe. He states that the earth will be "broken up" in the western portion of America. Scientists for many years have said that the San Andreas fault in California was overdue for an earthquake, so any changes there would not come as a big surprise. Cayce also says that the "greater portion" of Japan must go into the sea. This fits perfectly with what geologists know about the nature of the earth's crust around Japan. This part of the crust (called a tectonic plate) is gradually dipping under another section of crust and is therefore called a subduction zone. Geologists believe this subduction will take millions of years, but Cayce seems to imply that it will happen much sooner.

The reading states that these changes will *begin* in the period '58 to '98. It also says that the frigid and semitropical areas of the earth will become warmer, and that this will begin in the time period between 1958 to 1998. This is just when we began to dump trillions of tons of CO_2 into the atmosphere, and the polar ice cap began to melt.

The phrase "changed as in the twinkling of an eye" suggests an immediate change for northern Europe. This could be the destruction of dikes in the Netherlands, which would flood a great deal of land in a very short time, since much of the Netherlands is below sea level. This comes to mind as the most vulnerable spot for earthquake destruction in Europe.

Part of this reading says that land will appear off the east coast of America. Cayce followers believe that this may have already happened with the birth of the volcanic island Surtsey in the Atlantic Ocean. If they are interpreting the reading correctly, part of Cayce's prophecy may have already been fulfilled. Surtsey rose right out of the ocean floor, formed by cooling lava, so in that sense it just "appeared."

Cayce gave another reading about earth changes that makes some very startling predictions about the changes that will occur in the United States:

As to conditions in the geography of the world, of the country— changes here are gradually coming about. No wonder, then, that the entity feels the need, the necessity for change of central location. For, many portions of the east coast will be disturbed, as well as many portions of the west coast, as well as the central portion of the U.S. In the next few years lands will appear in the Atlantic as well as in the Pacific. And what is the coast line now of many a land will be the bed of the ocean.

Even many of the battlefields of the present will be ocean, will be the seas, the bays, the lands over which the NEW order will carry on their trade as one with another.

Portions of the now east coast of New York, or New York City itself, will in the main disappear. This will be another generation, though, here; while the southern portions of Carolina, Georgia— these will disappear. This will be much sooner.

The waters of the lakes will empty into the Gulf rather than the waterway over which such discussions have been recently made. It would be well if the waterway were prepared, but not for that purpose for which it is at present being considered.

Then the area where the entity is now located [Virginia Beach] will be among the safety lands, as will be portions of what is now Ohio, Indiana and Illinois, and much of the southern portion of Canada and the eastern portion of Canada; while the western land—much of that is to be disturbed—in this land—as, of course, much in other lands . . .

Q. I have for many months felt that I should move away from New York City.

A. This is well, as indicated. There is too much unrest; there will continue to be the character of vibrations that to the body will be disturbing, and eventually those destruction forces there—though these will be in the next generation.

Q. Will Los Angeles be safe?

A. Los Angeles, San Francisco, most of all these will be among those that will be destroyed before New York even.

Q. Should California or Virginia Beach be considered at all, or where is the right place that God has already provided for me to live?

A. As indicated, these choices should be made rather in self. Virginia Beach or the area is much safer as a definite place. But the work of the entity should embrace most all of the areas from the east to the west coast, in its persuading—not as a preacher, nor as one bringing a message of doom, but as a loving warning to all groups, clubs, woman's clubs, writer's clubs, art groups, those of every form of club, that there needs be—in their activities—definite work towards the knowledge of men . . .

Q. Is Virginia Beach to be safe?

A. It is the center—and the only seaport and center—of the White Brotherhood. 1152-11

In this reading Cayce says that portions of the east coast will be disturbed as well as the west coast. He even predicts the destruction of New York City. What form this destruction will take is not spelled out, but the use of the word "disappear" seems to imply that it will be covered by the ocean. This disappearance is mentioned right after he says that the "coast line now of many a land" will be the bed of the ocean. Included in this submergence are the battlefields of World War II, which would include the coastlands of Europe. The oceans would only have to rise a few feet to cover much of what is now the coastland of many countries in Europe and elsewhere. Global warming is causing the temperature of the earth to rise and making the north polar ice cap melt at a rate of 4% per decade. Once the ice cap melts this will raise the temperature of the Arctic, and the Greenland ice cap will melt as well. This would raise world seal levels, and the ocean would cover the areas Cayce mentions in his readings. It is amazing that Cayce predicted global warming and the resulting effects decades before it began to happen.

There may be another cause of New York's destruction, however. Very few people are aware that there is an earthquake fault running right through the center of New York City. It is inactive at this time, but it might be activated by the earth changes.

Other changes are mentioned in this reading, including the disappearance of the southern portions of Georgia and the Carolinas. These areas, like New York City, are only a few feet above sea level and would be in danger of being covered by a rising ocean. In fact, southern Georgia and South Carolina were once the bottom of the ocean, and to this day have sandy soil from the deposits that occurred at that time.

One question we could ask is why would Virginia Beach be safe when other portions of the east coast will not? One possible reason is that the earth's crust around Virginia Beach is rising at the present time. During the last Ice Age the weight of the continental glacier that covered much of the United States caused the crust around Virginia Beach to sink, and the crust is just now recoiling from that sinkage. Perhaps during the earth changes whatever direction the earth's crust is heading will be accelerated, pushing Virginia Beach up even more.

Other safety areas mentioned are Indiana, Illinois, and southern and eastern Canada. This matches geological evidence, since Indiana and Illinois are very stable areas, and the rock crust in Canada is so hard that geologists refer to it as the "Canadian shield," the most geologically stable area in the world. This reading does state, however, that the waters of the Great Lakes will empty into the Gulf of Mexico, rather than the Atlantic via the St. Lawrence Seaway. Current geological trends show that the crust around the St. Lawrence Seaway is tilting back toward the Great Lakes and will one day cause the Lakes to empty into the Gulf. Geologists say that this will not happen for many thousands of years, but the trend may be accelerated by a pole shift.

The most disturbing part of this reading is that Cayce states that San Francisco and Los Angeles will be destroyed before

New York. Given what we know about the earthquake activity in California, one does not have to be a psychic to predict this. Several major earthquakes occur each century along the San Andreas fault, and San Francisco and Los Angeles are built dangerously close to the fault. Cayce states that the predictions for the destruction of these cities should be given as a "loving warning" and not as a "message of doom," but one must admit that these predictions are indeed gloomy.

For those who don't think major earth changes could occur in the central United States, consider the Missouri earthquake of December 16, 1811. It was the most powerful quake in United States history and was felt over a million square miles. It changed the course of the Mississippi River, creating new islands and lakes. Naturalist John J. Audubon stated that "the earth waved like a field of corn before the breeze." Eliza Bryan, a pioneer, described it as follows: "About 2 o'clock a.m. a violent shock of earthquake accompanied by a very awful noise resembling loud but distance thunder, but hoarse and vibrating, followed by complete saturation of the atmosphere with sulphurous vapor, causing total darkness." The Mississippi River actually stopped, rolled backward, and then surged ahead in huge tidal waves.

The most interesting point regarding this awesome destruction is that the earthquake caused total darkness. The sun's darkening predicted in the Bible may be caused by an earthquake as powerful.

Another interesting point about the earthquake in Missouri is that it created "earthquake Christians." People were so awestruck by the power of the quake and the threat of sudden death that they turned to religion. It has been said that "there are no atheists in foxholes," and apparently there are no atheists during earthquakes either.

Cayce tells us in the following reading that there will be a purpose behind the earth changes:

Ye say that these are of the sea; yes—for there shall the breaking up be, until there are those in every land that shall say that this or that shows the hand of divine interference, or that it is nature taking a hand, or that it is the natural consequence of good judgments. 3976-26

Cayce once again mentions the "breaking up" and says that it will show the "hand of divine interference." One of the Dead Sea Scrolls entitled the "Battle of the Sons of Light and Darkness" speaks of the "Sons of Darkness" being destroyed during the end time by a "hand not of man." This might be a reference to the destruction of the invader of the Middle East by natural means such as an earthquake, much as Jericho in the Bible was destroyed. Of course, Cayce's comment on the "natural consequence of good judgments" is a reference to the building of cities on earthquake faults—San Francisco and Los Angeles being the most obvious examples. Humanity should know better than to build cities in seismically active areas, for sooner or later a major quake will strike. The destruction would seem inevitable even without the coming earth changes. However, people through their actions can have an effect on the earth. Exploding nuclear devices underground and pumping oil out of the ground near earthquake faults will cause the changes to be more severe. We should realize this. On the positive side, Cayce repeatedly stated that a small group of people praying together could save a city, a state, or a region. He emphasized that some of the predictions he made were trends, and that the will of humankind could change the future. Cayce predicted earth changes for northern Alabama in the 1930s that did not occur, so it is probable that people in that area raised their consciousness in such a way as to keep the destruction from happening. Cayce has not been infallible in his predictions of earth changes. Certainly the omens predicted in the Bible will happen regardless of the actions of humans; however, we can have an effect on our own destiny.

The Return of Jesus

The following section of the Bible describes Jesus' ascension into heaven from Mount Olives after the resurrection:

Acts 1:9-12

And when he had spoken these things, while they beheld, he was taken up, and a cloud received him out of their sight. And while they looked steadfastly toward heaven as he went up, behold, two men stood by them in white apparel; Who said, men of Galilee, why do you stand gazing up into heaven? This same Jesus, who is taken up from you into heaven, shall so come in like manner as you have seen him go into heaven. Then they returned to Jerusalem from the Mount called Olives which is from Jerusalem a sabbath day's journey.

Jesus ascends from the top of Mount Olives into heaven and is received by a cloud. Two men in white standing alongside tell the men of Galilee that Jesus will return "in like manner. "The phrase, "in like manner," literally means in exactly the same manner. This means that Jesus will return to Mount Olives, descending exactly as he ascended. Mount Olives is very close to Jerusalem, and the appearance of Jesus there will be seen all over the city; thus his reappearance will be apparent to all the world. To those familiar with the Bible his appearance will be anticipated. Now let's look at what Cayce says about Jesus' return:

Q. Is Jesus the Christ on any particular sphere or is He manifesting on the earth plane in another body?

A. As just given, all power in heaven, in earth, is given to Him who overcame. Hence He is of

Himself in space, in the force that impels through faith, through belief, in the individual entity. As a Spirit Entity. Hence not in a body in the earth, but may come at will to him who WILLS to be one with, and acts in love to make same possible. For, He shall come as ye have seen Him go, in the BODY He occupied in Galilee. The body that He formed, that was crucified on the cross, that rose from the tomb, that walked by the sea, that appeared to Simon, that appeared to Philip, that appeared to "I, even John." 5749-4

The first part of this reading has to do with Jesus as a spirit entity. Cayce tells us that anyone can be with the Christ spirit if he or she desires and acts in love to make it possible. The second part of this reading deals with the physical return of Jesus and even quotes a translation of the verses of Acts we just looked at, stating that Jesus will return even as the men of Galilee saw Him go. So Cayce agrees with the Bible that Jesus will return in the flesh to Mount Olives. He will occupy the same body He did before, the body that was crucified and rose from the tomb. He will be recognized as Jesus, and so Cayce is definitely speaking of a physical return. These next readings emphasize this point even more:

Q. What is meant by "the day of the Lord is near at hand"?

A. That as has been promised through the prophets and the sages of old, the time—and half time—has been and is being fulfilled in this day and generation . . .

Q. How soon?

A. When those that are His have made the way clear, PASSABLE, for Him to come. 262-49

Keep the faith that ye are magnified in the Persian experience, as ye sought for Him who is the light, the hope of the world today. For until there is again the seeking of such as ye not only proclaimed but manifested, he CANNOT come again. 1908-1

The quote from the Bible Book of Acts is once again emphasized. Another point is added: Jesus cannot come again until those that are "His" have made the way passable. This point is explained in reading 1908-1 by the fact that there must be the seeking of the Christ Spirit before Jesus will return. This seeking will be the attracting principle that will bring Jesus back to earth. Like attracts like. This is explained in the following readings:

Q. He said He would come again. What about His second coming?

A. The time no one knows. Even as He gave, not even the Son Himself. ONLY the Father. Not until His enemies—and the earth—are wholly in subjection to His will. His powers.

Q. Are we entering the period of preparation for His coming?

A. Entering the test period, rather. 5749-2

Q. When Jesus the Christ comes the second time, will He set up His kingdom on earth and will it be an everlasting kingdom?

A. Read His promises in that ye have written of His words, even as "I gave." He shall rule for a thousand years. Then shall Satan be loosed again for a season. 5749-4

Q. Please explain what is meant by "He will walk and talk with men of every clime." Does this mean He will appear to many at once or appear to various people during a long period?

A. As given, for a thousand years He will walk and talk with men of every clime. Then in groups, in masses, and then they shall reign of the first resurrection for a thousand years; for this will be when the changes materially come . . .

Q. In the Persian experience as San (or Zend) did Jesus give the basic teachings of what became Zoroastrianism?

A. In all those periods that the basic principle was the Oneness of the Father, He has walked with men. 364-8

He will not tarry, for having overcome He shall appear even AS the Lord AND Master. Not as one born, but as one that returneth to His own, for He will walk and talk with men of every clime, and those that are faithful and just in their reckoning shall be caught up with Him to rule and to do JUDGMENT for a thousand years! 364-7

We can see from these readings that Jesus will not return until the whole earth is in subjection to his will. This is certainly not the case today, and it will take a powerful stimulus for this to occur. But once again, Cayce states that the earth must be ready for him if he is to return. I believe the key to this change in consciousness by the people of the earth will be the darkening of the sun. It is one of the most important omens—mentioned repeatedly in the Bible as preceding the return of Jesus. It is written in the Koran, so it will be recognized universally as proof of his return. Signs such as this will be so incredible that people all over the earth will have only one place to turn for help, to God. The power of millions of people praying will create an attraction that will draw Jesus back to the earth.

Mentioned in all four of the previous readings are the thousand years of peace that will follow Jesus' return. This is referred to as the "millennium" by the fundamentalists and the "Age of Aquarius" by the New Age people. It will be a period of time unparalleled in human history. Evil will be set aside, and peace on earth will be the rule.

The book of Revelation also says that Satan will be locked up for a thousand years, after which time he will be released "for a season." Those allowed to incarnate during this time will be only those who have not worshiped the animal influences. All of humanity will realize and accept the existence of God. There will be no more war or hatred. In short it will be the greatest time in human history.

A Physical Description of Jesus

When Jesus returns, how will we know him? What will he look like? Unknown to most people there is a physical description of Jesus in the archives of Rome. This description is contained in a report written two thousand years ago by a Roman, Publius Lentulus, to the Emperor Tiberias:

"There has appeared in Palestine a man who is still living and whose power is extraordinary. He has the title given him of Great Prophet; his disciples call him the Son of God. He raises the dead and heals all sorts of diseases. "He is a tall, well-proportioned man, and there is an air of severity in his countenance which at once attracts the love and reverence of those who see him. His hair is the color of new wine from the roots to the ears, and thence to the shoulders, it is curled and falls down to the lowest part of them. Upon the forehead, it parts in two after the manner of

Nazarenes. "His forehead is flat and fair, his face without blemish or defect, and adorned with a graceful expression. His nose and mouth are very well proportioned, his beard is thick and the color of his hair. His eyes are gray and extremely lively.

"In his reproofs, he is terrible, but his exhortations and instructions, amiable and courteous. There is something wonderfully charming in his face with a mixture of gravity. He is never seen to laugh, but has been observed to weep [Cayce says He did laugh and quite often]. He is very straight in stature, his hands large and spreading, his arms are very beautiful. He talks little, but with a great quality and is the handsomest man in the world."

The description of Jesus in the Cayce readings agrees with the one above:

... a vision of the Master as might be put on canvas ... [would] be entirely different from all these which have been depicted of the face, the body, the eyes, the cut of the chin and the lack entirely of the Jewish or Aryan profile. For these were clear, clean, ruddy, hair almost like that of David, a golden brown, yellow-red ... 5354-1

The Master's hair is 'most red, inclined to be curly in portions, yet not feminine or weak—STRONG, with heavy piercing eyes that are blue or steel-gray. 5749-1

In other readings we are told that Jesus wore a pearl gray robe. So a complete picture of Jesus would be of a tall, well-proportioned man wearing a pearl gray robe and having reddish brown hair and steel-gray eyes. This is what Jesus will look like when he returns.

THE GREAT PYRAMID AND THE SPHINX

According to the Cayce readings, during the last part of this century humankind will make the greatest archaeological discovery of all time. This discovery will involve the Egyptian pyramids at Gizeh. The Great Pyramid and the Sphinx will yield treasures beyond the wildest dream of any Egyptologist.

The story of Gizeh goes back many thousands of years, before the Great Flood of Noah's time. During those ancient times, according to the readings, a king by the name of Arart moved his tribe into the Nile Valley and conquered the natives there. Arart's spiritual leader was a priest by the name of Ra Ta. Inspired from on high, Ra Ta conceived a spiritual monument to last for all time, what is now known as the Great Pyramid at Gizeh. Hermes, who is often mentioned in Egyptian legends, was the architect of the project:

. . . the entering in of Hermes WITH Ra—who came as one of the peoples from the mount to which these peoples had been banished . . . Hence under the authority of Ra, and Hermes as the guide, or the actual (as would be termed in the present) constructing or construction architect with the priest or Ra giving the directions . . .294-151

Arart's son, Araaraart, was king at the time of the completion of the project, which is much older than generally believed.

Q. What was the date of the actual beginning and ending of the construction of the Great Pyramid?

A. Was one hundred years in construction. Begun and completed in the period of Araaraart's time, with Hermes and Ra.

Q. What was the date B.C. of that period?

A. 10,490 to 10,390 before the Prince entered into Egypt. 5748-6

The Great Pyramid was built by the use of forces we are only now beginning to rediscover.

Q. How was this particular Great Pyramid of Gizeh built?

A. By the use of those forces in nature as make for iron to swim. Stone floats in the air in the same manner. This will be discovered in '58. 5748-6

Q. By what power or powers were these early pyramids and temples constructed?

A. By the lifting forces of those gases that are being used gradually in the present civilization, and by the fine work or activities of those versed in that pertaining to the source from which all power comes. 5750-1

The force in nature that causes "iron to swim" is buoyancy. Buoyancy has been known since the time of Archimedes, but the method for focusing this force was not known until 1958 and still isn't totally understood.

Many important discoveries were made in 1958 including the invention of the laser. Since the readings say that the Atlanteans aided in the construction of the Pyramid and since the readings also say that the principal source of power for the Atlantean civilization was light focused on a crystal, the laser may have been the method by which the forces of buoyancy were controlled.

For there was not only the adding to the monuments, but the Atlanteans aided in their activities with the creating of that called the Pyramid, with its records of events of the earth through its activity in all ages to that in which the new dispensation is to come. 281-43

The Great Pyramid was constructed in a manner such that it would be difficult, if not impossible, to reproduce it today. It contains 2,300,000 stones, many weighing as much as 20 tons. Its blocks are fitted together so finely that a razor blade cannot fit between the blocks of the Great Pyramid. The technology used in its construction is superior to ours today because it was built by Atlanteans.

According to the readings, the continent of Atlantis existed for thousands of years at a state of technology far beyond what we have today. But because of the misuse of this technology, the continent began to break up and sink into what is now the Atlantic Ocean. The total destruction took place over many years, and some Atlanteans escaped and found their way to Egypt and the Nile Valley.

Egyptologists would say that this story is pure fantasy, but several facts dispute this. The large pyramids in Egypt were allegedly tombs for ancient Pharaohs, yet no bodies have ever been found in any of the larger pyramids. Grave robbers are always cited as the reason for this, but to reach the King's Chamber of the Great Pyramid, explorers had to dig around a 29-foot granite plug. When they reached the King's Chamber, it was empty. If grave robbers had been there before the exploration, would they have plugged the passage with a 29-foot-thick granite stone to protect an empty tomb?

The priest Ra and Hermes incorporated mathematics into the Pyramid, including the relationship of pi and phi. This clearly shows that their knowledge of science was greater than that believed to be possessed by ancient humanity. These mathematical relations were not supposed to have been discovered until much later.

Geographical considerations also went into the building of the Great Pyramid:

When the lines about the earth are considered from the mathematical precisions, it will be found that the center is nigh unto where the Great Pyramid, which was begun then, is still located. 281-42

At the correct time accurate imaginary lines can be drawn from the opening of the great Pyramid to the second star in the Great Dipper, called Polaris or the North Star. This indicates it is the system toward which the soul takes its flight after having completed its sojourn through this solar system. 5748-6

The Great Pyramid is arranged in a perfect north-south alignment, so close that after thousands of years it is off axis by only an inch or so. The entrance to the inner chambers is on an angle that faces directly toward Polaris. This indicates that each soul goes to that system after completing the cycle in this solar system. This is one of the more esoteric messages built into the Great Pyramid.

Much has been written in recent years of the special properties of the pyramid shape itself. Books about "pyramid power" have testified to the ability of pyramids to do everything from sharpening razor blades to mummifying fruit. These effects are caused by the ability of the pyramid to focus cosmic energy. A pyramid can do this because it is a model of three-dimensional reality. If you take a two-dimensional square and use only one point to make it a three-dimensional object, the result is a pyramid. The Great Pyramid focuses cosmic energy by mirroring three-dimensional reality in on itself, in the same way that opposing mirrors make smaller and smaller images of each other into infinity.

The ability to focus energy is even contained in the name "pyramid." "Pyra" comes from the word for fire, "pyro"; and "mid" means middle. So "pyramid" means "fire in the middle" or a focus of cosmic energy.

The Great Pyramid is built largely of limestone blocks that are made of small crystals. Limestone crystals are known for their even vibration and were chosen in order to focus the Pyramid's vibrations evenly. More will undoubtedly be learned about pyramid energy in the future as it is studied by modern-day science.

Not only is the Great Pyramid a focus of energy but it incorporates in its stones and inner passages the history and future of humanity:

. . . the rise and fall of the nations were to be depicted in this same temple that was to act as an interpreter for that which had been, that which is, and that which is to be, in the material plane.

294-151

This, then, receives all the records from the beginnings of that given by the priest, Arart, Araaraart and Ra, to that period when there is to be the change in the earth's position and the return of the Great Initiate to that and other lands for the folding up of those prophecies that are depicted there. All changes that came in the religious thought in the world are shown there, in the variations in which the passage through same is reached, from the base

to the top—or to the open tomb AND the top. These are signified by both the layer and the color in what direction the turn is made. 5748-5

The rise and fall of nations are depicted in the Great Pyramid along with the changes in religious thought which will come about in the world. This can be seen by examining the passages. The first passage is descending, and this undoubtedly represents the fall of humankind from grace. The next passage is ascending, which represents our ascent from the birth of Jesus to the present age. The stone prophecies continue until the return of the Great Initiate, Jesus, at the end of this age.

During Jesus' studies in Egypt, the Great Pyramid was used as a Hall of Initiation for Him and John the Baptist into the knowledge of One God:

Then, with Hermes and Ra (those that assumed or took up the work of Araaraart) there began the building of that now called Gizeh, with which those prophecies that had been in the Temple of Records and the Temple Beautiful were builded, in the building of this that was to be the hall of the initiates of that sometimes referred to as the White Brotherhood. 5748-5

In this same pyramid did the Great Initiate, the Master, take those last of the Brotherhood degrees with John, the forerunner of Him, at that place. 5748-5

This initiation involved breaking the cycle of death and rebirth, which Jesus did so dramatically with His resurrection. The initiation in the Great Pyramid was a symbolic prelude to this.

Q. Please describe Jesus' initiation in Egypt, telling if the Gospel reference to "three days and nights in the grave or tomb," possibly in the shape of a cross, indicate a special initiation.

A. This is a portion of the initiation—it is a part of the passage through that to which each soul is to attain in its development, as has the world through each period of their incarnation in the earth. As is supposed, the record of the earth through the passage through the tomb, or the pyramid, is that through which each entity, each soul, as an initiate must pass for the attaining to the releasing of same—as indicated by the empty tomb, which has NEVER been filled, see? Only Jesus was able to break same, as it became that which indicated His fulfillment. 2067-70

Each soul in the earth plane must pass through the same sort of initiation in order to break the death cycle. Part of this initiation will be the darkness that will overcome the sun before Jesus' return. A more important part will be the recognition by everyone that death is not the end of life.

Of the prophecies represented in the Great Pyramid Cayce mentions several specifically:

Q. Are the deductions and conclusions arrived at by D. Davidson and H. Aldersmith in their book on The Great Pyramid correct?

A. Many of these that have been taken as deductions are correct. Many are far overdrawn.

Only an initiate may understand.

Q. What corrections for the period of the 20th century?

A. Only those that there will be an upheaval in '36.

Q. Do you mean there will be an upheaval in '36 as recorded in the pyramid?

A. As recorded in the pyramid, though this is set for a correction, which, as has been given, is between '32 AND '38—the correction would be, for this—as seen—is '36—for it is in many—these run from specific days; for, as has been seen, there are periods when even the hour, day, year, place, country, nation, town, and individuals are pointed out. That's how correct are many of those prophecies as made. 5748-5

According to Edgar Cayce, some of the prophecies in the Great Pyramid are correct as to the hour, day, year, place, country, nation, town, and individuals involved. This got me thinking, how can you build a monument to predict an hour, day, year, place, country, nation, town, and individuals involved 12,000 years into the future?

They did this in a very clever way. The Sphinx and the Great Pyramid were built in the astrological Age of Leo. Leo's symbol is the lion. The prophecies will be fulfilled at the beginning of the Age of Aquarius. Aquarius' symbol is the man pouring a pitcher of water. The Sphinx has the body of a lion, which represents the Age of Leo, and the head of a man, which represents the Age of Aquarius. So the Sphinx represents the 12,000 years of history between the Age of Leo and the Age of Aquarius.

Cayce discusses other prophecies in the following reading:

A great deal in various experiences of same; that is, in the interpreting of periods of those activities which preceded that period in which the building was begun there. For, remember, this was not an interpretation only from that period FORWARD, but as to the very PLACE and experience in which there is to be the change in the activities in the earth! 849-45

Q. What are the correct interpretations of the indications in the Great Pyramid regarding the time when the present depression will end?

A. The changes as indicated and outlined are for the latter part of the present year (1932). As far as depression is concerned, this is not—as in the minds of many—because fear has arisen, but rather that, when fear has arisen in the hearts of the created, sin lieth at the door. Then, the change will occur—or that seeking will make the definite change—in the latter portion of the present year. Not that times financially will be better but the minds of the people will be fitted to the conditions better.

Q. What will be the type and extent of the upheaval in '36?

A. The wars, the upheavals in the interior of the earth, and the shifting of same by the differentiation in the axis as respecting the positions from the Polaris center. 5748-6

Two types of upheavals are discussed in this reading, wars and changes in the interior of the earth that will cause the poles to shift. The year 1936 was a turning point for World War II, since it was the year that Hitler became aggressive and marched into the Rhineland. At that time German armed forces were still weak, and if the Allies had resisted, Hitler's dominance of Europe might have been prevented. Also, 1936 was the beginning of the Spanish Civil War, which became a mini version of the larger war to come, with Fascism fighting democracy.

The upheaval within the earth that occurred in 1936 was apparently at the earth's core and will take time to work its way out. This is understandable since the earth is a revolving mass of molten nickel and iron, whose only solid portion is the thin layer of crust we live on. When a spinning top develops a slight wobble, it takes time to topple over, and the earth is no exception. A slight shift in equilibrium can gradually become a larger one.

Somehow the pole shift is represented in the stones of the Great Pyramid, and the following reading seems to imply that the constellation of Libra is involved:

[The Great Pyramid] was to be the presentation of that which had been gained by these peoples through the activities of Ra Ta, who NOW was known as Ra . . . [and] there was brought the idea of the preservation of these, not only for those in the present but for the generations that were to come in the experiences and experiences throughout that period, until the changes were to come again in the earth's position . . . It was formed according to that which had been worked out by Ra Ta in the mount as related to the position of the various stars, that acted in the place about which this particular solar system circles in its activity, going towards what? That same name as to which the priest was banished—the constellation of Libra, or to Libya were these peoples sent. 294-151

It may be that the poles will shift toward Libra, or it may be that the whole solar system will shift. The reading is not clear. Cayce may have been referring to the earth and the moon as a "system." One thing that is known is that all the stars in the galaxy are constantly shifting position, and our sun and the pole star, Polaris, are no exceptions. Neither are the earth and the moon.

Of all the prophecies depicted in the Great Pyramid one of the most important has to do with the so-called King's Chamber at the top of the interior passageways. In the King's Chamber is an empty sarcophagus or coffin.

Q. What definite details are indicated as to what will happen after we enter the period of the King's

Chamber?

A. When the bridegroom is at hand, all do rejoice. When we enter that understanding of being in the King's presence, with that of the mental seeking, the joy, the buoyancy, the new understanding, the new life, through the period.

Q. What is the significance of the empty sarcophagus?

A. That there will be no more death. Don't misunderstand or misinterpret! But the INTERPRETATION of death will be made plain.

Q. What is the date, as recorded by the Pyramid, of entering in the King's Chamber?

A. '38 to '58. 5748-6

The entity saw what was preserved as the memorials, the pyramids built during the entity's sojourn; when there was begun the pyramid of understanding or Gizeh—and only to the king's chamber was the pathway built. But the entity will see in the present the empty tomb period pass; hence rise to heights of activity in the present experience. 275-33

The meaning of the empty sarcophagus is that the death of the physical body does not mean the death of the soul. The prophecy connected with this is the return of the bridegroom, Jesus (as He is symbolized in the Bible), and the realization by the whole human race that the spirit survives death. This was the purpose of Jesus' resurrection, to allow a way for us to overcome death and to show that death could be overcome.

Above the empty sarcophagus in the King's Chamber are seven stones. These stones are arranged in the fashion of an arrow, with five stones as the shaft and two stones as the tip. This symbolizes the raising of energy through the seven endocrine centers. When you enter the King's Chamber you say, "Where has the body gone?" It has ascended upward through the seven centers out of the physical plane. Remember that Cayce said that the King's Chamber represented the "changes that came in the religious thought in the world." (5748-5)

The most important change in religious thought will be the realization that the seven endocrine centers are the key to spiritual development. And the arrow points the way upward.

The five lower stones in the arrow are made of red granite and represent the five lower centers of the body (thus the color red is used). The two stones at the top are made of gray limestone and represent the pineal and pituitary glands, which are gray. The top two stones are connected, as the pituitary and pineal are connected by the thalamus and the hypothalamus. Even more esoteric is the fact that limestone was used. Lime accumulates in the brain such that years ago physicians called lime salts "brain sand." Also, the pituitary and pineal regulate the amount of lime in the body, so limestone was a perfect symbol for the two higher glands.

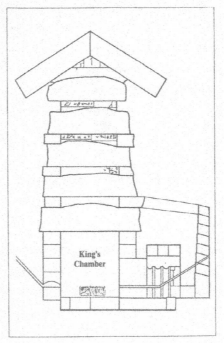

The seven stones above the King's Chamber.

On the back of every U.S. dollar bill is a pyramid with an eye in the middle of it. The "eye in the pyramid" symbolizes the pineal or third eye of the body in beautifully mystical fashion. This eye also represents the seven stones above the empty sarcophagus, making one of the United States' most common symbols a very esoteric one.

Next to the Great Pyramid of Gizeh is a monument the readings often call the mystery of mysteries, the Sphinx.

Until recent times the Sphinx has been covered by sand up to its neck, but as the time draws near for the Sphinx to reveal its secrets, the whole body of the Sphinx has been uncovered.

It is more than just a symbol, however, because for thousands of years the Sphinx has been guarding a storehouse of historical records known as the Hall of Records. This Hall of Records, buried beneath the sands of Gizeh, contains the history of humankind from the beginning, including the rise and fall of Atlantis.

The entity aided in those activities, being among the children of the Law of One from Atlantis; AIDING the Priest in that preparation, in that manner of building the temples of records that lie just beyond that enigma that still is the mystery of mysteries to those who seek to know what were the manners of thought of the ancient sons who made man—a beast—as a part of the consciousness. 2402-2

In the information as respecting the pyramids, their purpose in the experience of the peoples, in the period when there was the rebuilding of the priest during the return in the land, some 10,500 before the coming of the Christ into the land, there was first that attempt to restore and add to that which had been begun on what is called the Sphinx, and the treasure or storehouse facing same, between this and the Nile, in which those records were kept by Arart and Araaraart in the period. 5748-5

These records, when they are found, will constitute the most incredible archaeological find of all time. They contain not only the history of Atlantis but all of its spiritual truths that have been lost to us for thousands of years.

Q. In which pyramid or temple are the records mentioned in the readings given through this channel on Atlantis, in April, 1932 [(364) series]?

A. As given, that temple was destroyed at the time there was the last destruction of Atlantis. Yet, as time draws nigh when changes are to come about, there may be the opening of those three places where the records are one, to those that are the initiates in the knowledge of the One God: The temple by Iltar will then rise again. Also there will be the opening of the temple or hall of records in Egypt, and those records that were put into the heart of the Atlantean land may also be found there—that have been kept for those that are of that group. The RECORDS are ONE. 5750-1

. . . these were to be kept as had been given by the priests in Atlantis or Poseidia (Temple), when these records of the race of the developments, of the laws pertaining to One were put in their chambers . . . 378-16

The laws of One are the laws having to do with One God and were given by the priests in Atlantis to be preserved in the Hall of Records. However, there are two other places where the records are also preserved—in the temple of Iltar near the Yucatan in Mexico and underwater off the coast of what is now Bimini. These two locations were given in another reading. In those three places "The RECORDS are ONE."

The records are not in any language with which we are familiar but are written in a combination of Egyptian and Atlantean letters.

The entity was a priestess in the Law of One, and among those who—ill—came into the Egyptian land—as the elders in those groups for preserving the records, as well as for preserving a portion of that race, that peoples.

With the periods of reconstruction after the return of the Priest, the entity joined with those who were active in putting the records in forms that were partially of the old characters of the ancient or early Egyptian, part in the newer form of the Atlanteans. These may be found, especially when the house or tomb of records is opened, in a few years from now. 2537-1

Q. Give in detail what the sealed room contains.

A. A record of Atlantis from the beginning of those periods when the Spirit took form or began the encasements in that land, and the developments of the peoples throughout their sojourn, with the records of the first destruction and the changes that took place in the land, with the record of the

SOJOURNINGS of the peoples to the varied activities in other lands, and a record of the meetings of all the nations or lands for the activities in the destructions that became necessary with the final destruction of Atlantis and the buildings of the pyramid of initiation, with who, what, where, would come the opening of the records that are as copies from the sunken Atlantis; for with the change it must rise (the temple) again.

This in position lies, as the sun rises from the waters, the line of the shadow (or light) falls between the paws of the Sphinx, that was later set as the sentinel or guard, and which may not be entered from the connecting chambers from the Sphinx's paw (right paw) until the TIME has been fulfilled when the changes must be active in this sphere of man's experience.

Between, then, the Sphinx and the river.

378-16

According to Cayce, the records also contain a prophecy of who will find them, when this will happen, and where they will be found. The connecting chambers will be opened from the Sphinx's right paw, and this gives us a tremendous clue as to where the entrance to the Hall of Records is. Of course, people familiar with the readings have examined the Sphinx's right paw for years, and the entrance has not yet been found, but there may be a helpful clue in the following reading:

Q. In what capacity did this entity act regarding the building of the sphinx?

A. As the monuments were being rebuilt in the plains of that now called the pyramid of Gizeh, this entity builded, laid, the foundations; that is, superintended same, figured out the geometrical position of same in relation to those buildings as were put up of that connecting the sphinx. And the data concerning same may be found in the vaults in the base of the sphinx. We see this sphinx was builded as this:

The excavations were made for same in the plains above where the temple of Isis had stood during the deluge, occurring some centuries before, when this people (and this entity among them) came in from the north country and took possession of the rule of this country, setting up the first dynasty. The entity was with that dynasty, also in the second dynasty of Araaraart, when those buildings were begun. The base of the sphinx was laid out in channels, and in the corner facing the Gizeh may be found the wording of how this was founded, giving the history of the first invading ruler and the ascension of Araaraart to that position. 195-14

This reading tells us that at the corner base of the Sphinx facing Gizeh (the Great Pyramid) is the wording of how the Sphinx was founded and the history of Arart and his son Araaraart. On this corner of the Sphinx is a small rectangle about ten feet high, which

I call a "box." Located on the other side of the Sphinx near the right forepaw is another identical box.

One of these boxes of stone is by the corner facing the Great Pyramid, where records are located, according to Cayce, and the other box is by the right forepaw where the entrance to the Hall of Records is located. It may be a coincidence, but these boxes are located right where Cayce says there are underground chambers. Also significant is that no mention is made in any of the hieroglyphs concerning these boxes. Why? Perhaps they were to remain a secret until the time was ripe.

In the 1920s when the Sphinx was dug out of the sand, a statue of the Egyptian god of the underworld was found in pieces on top of the box by the right forepaw. Legend has it that a Pharaoh dismantled the box and discovered an underground passage leading from it. When his men went into the passage, they came out covered with painful sores. The Pharaoh had the box sealed and a statue of the god of the underworld placed on top of it. If this legend is true, the Pharaoh's men may have discovered the entrance to the Hall of Records, and then sealed it back up.

In 1982 S.R.I., Inc. (formerly Stanford Research Institute), did acoustical soundings underneath the right front paw of the Sphinx, and what they found is very interesting. Under the entire length of the right paw, they got a good clear signal, indicating there are no underground passages there. But directly under the right front paw box, the signal was dead in three places, as though some kind of opening or empty space were blocking the signal. These dead spots may be the passageway that the Pharaoh's men found.

The Sphinx's right front forepaw "box."   Photo by Uwe E. Wilken

When Cayce was alive, he did a series of readings for a man he said would be one of the ones to rediscover the Hall of Records. During the building of the Great Pyramid this man lived in Egypt, and his name at that time was Hept-supht. According to Cayce, Hept-supht means "keep it shut." He was in charge of closing up the records and keeping them shut until the time was right. He asked Cayce the following question:

Q. Am I the one to receive directions as to where the sealed room is and how to find it?

A. One of the two. Two with a guide. Heptsupht, El-ka[?], and Atlan. These will appear. 378-16

Since the man asking the question died in 1960, it is apparent that he will make the discovery during a more recent incarnation, one that probably began in the last few years. Two others will appear to join him, Atlan and El-ka by their Atlantean names. Hept-supht will find the records because he was the one that sealed them thousands of years ago during an elaborate ceremony.

And, as this was to be (Gizeh we are speaking of) the place for the initiates and their gaining by personal application, and by the journey or journeys through the various activities—as in the ceremonial actions of those that became initiates, it became very fitting (to those as in Ra, and those of Ra-Ta Ra) that there should be the crowning or placing of this symbol of the record, and of the initiates' place of activity, by one who represented both the old and the new; one representing then the Sons of the Law in Atlantis, Lemuria, Oz and Og. So, he that keeps the record, that keeps shut, or Hept-supht, was made or chosen as the one to seal that in the tomb. The ceremony was long; the clanging of the apex by the gavel that was used in the sounding of the placing. Hence there has arisen from this ceremony many of those things that may be seen in the present; as the call to prayer, the church bell in the present, may be termed a descendant; the sounding of the trumpet as the call to arms, or that as revelry; the sound as of those that make for mourning, in the putting away of the body; the sounding as of ringing in the new year, the sounding as of the coming of the bridegroom; all have their inception from the sound that was made that kept the earth's record of the earth's building, as to that from the change. The old record in Gizeh is from that as recorded from the journey to Pyrenees; and to 1998 from the death of the Son of Man (as a man). 378-14

The following readings tell us when the records will be found:

As for the physical records—it will be necessary to wait until the full time has come for the breaking up of much that has been in the nature of selfish motives in the world. For, remember, these records were made from the angle of WORLD movements. So must thy activities be in the present of the universal approach, but as applied to the individual. 2329-3

**For, as must be known to all God IS! And the soul that becomes
more and more aware of His, God's use of man, that all may know
of His Presence, is becoming then in at-onement; as self was in
the experience, and preserved that record for the future entering
souls, that will be physically known when time has set its mark.
378-16**

**This may not be entered without an understanding, for those that
were left as guards may NOT be passed until after a period of their
regeneration in the Mount, or the fifth root race begins. 5748-6**

The records will not be found until there is the "breaking up of
. . . selfish motives in the world" and "time has set its mark." Clearly,
the selfish motives of the world will not be broken up until Jesus
returns, and so the opening of the Hall of Records will probably coin-
cide with that event. Humanity could not handle the technological
advances contained in the records without a spiritual understanding.

Cayce links the discovery of the records with the beginning
of the "fifth root race," and, according to the writings of Madam
Blavatsky, the fifth root race, or the change of humanity to a more
spiritual self, will not begin until Jesus returns.

Jesus said, "I will bring all things to thine remembrance." This
was not only a reference to the remembrance of past lives, but to the
revelation of humankind's history with the opening of the Hall of
Records.

The Shadow on the Great Pyramid

Cayce said that prophecies in the Great Pyramid were correct down to the specific day, place, and hour. But how do you
indicate a specific day, place, and hour, 12,000 years into the
future? The way the builders did this was very clever. On the

spring and fall equinoxes, the Great Pyramid and the Sphinx are perfectly aligned with the rising and setting sun. Why is this important? Because the Great Pyramid has eight sides. That's right, eight sides. This was discovered in 1940 when a British military plane flew over the Great Pyramid at sunset on the equinox and took a photograph which showed a shadow of one of the sides. Remarkably, this feature can only be seen from the air at sunrise or sunset on the spring or fall equinox. It is not visible at any other time of the year. The way the builders of the Great Pyramid accomplished this was by indenting the sides by 1%, so that the sun has to be perfectly aligned with the pyramid for the shadow to appear.

The pyramids at sunset on the equinox

The 8-Sided Great Pyramid

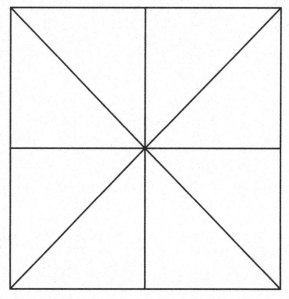

You can see the shadow in the photo of the Great Pyramid complex pictured here. The Great Pyramid is the one at the top of the photo. If you examine it closely, you can clearly see the shadow. But why did they build it this way? I believe they built it this way to tell us that a prophetic event will occur at sunrise or sunset on one of the equinoxes. But what event?

If you look at the second large pyramid in the photo, you can see it only has four sides. You can also see that the shadow of this pyramid is pointing directly to the right front forepaw of the Sphinx, which is where the entrance to the Hall of Records is located. I believe the builders built the pyramids this way to tell us that the Hall of Records was located there, and will be opened at sunrise or sunset on one of the equinoxes. In the last chapter of this book, we will examine which equinox that might be.

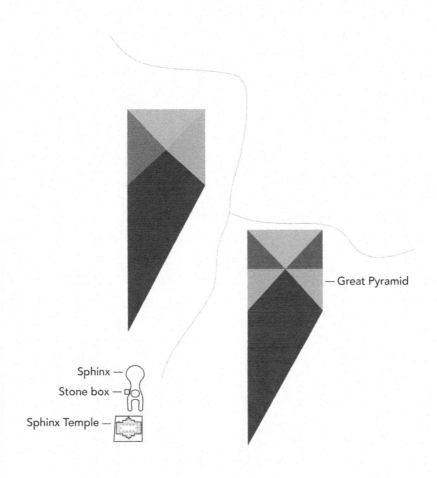

The shadow of the second pyramid points directly to the stone box at sunset on the equinox.

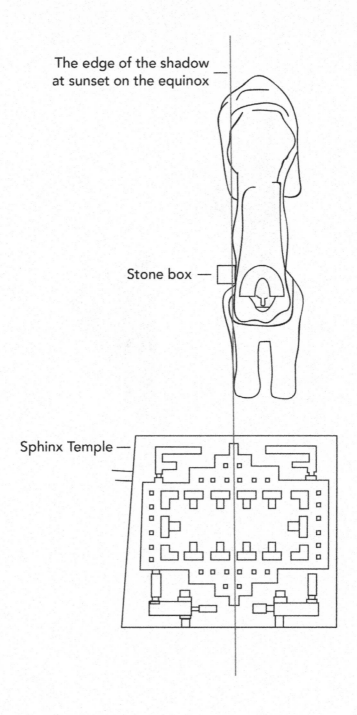

The edge of the shadow
at sunset on the equinox —

Stone box —

Sphinx Temple —

Jean-Pierre Houdin

In the late 1990's Jean-Pierre Houdin, a French architect, quit his job, sold his house, and moved into a small studio apartment to dedicate his life to trying to figure out how the Great Pyramid was built. After a year the French government caught wind of what Jean-Pierce was doing and gave him $100,000 and a small staff to help him work on the project. After four years Jean-Pierre had it worked out.

The first third of the Great Pyramid was built with a straight external ramp. The rest of the Pyramid was built with an internal, corkscrew-shaped ramp. The Grand Gallery in the interior of the Pyramid was used to haul some of the larger stones on a wooden sled with greased runners. Proof of Jean-Pierre's theory can still be seen in the Grand Gallery today, as the black marks from the grease are still visible on the walls.

Jean-Pierre then went on the lecture circuit to promote his idea. After one of his lectures he was approached by a scientist who was part of a French team that had surveyed the Great Pyramid in 1986 by measuring the strength of gravitational fields. The scientist showed Jean-Pierre a top down view of the survey that clearly showed the internal ramp.

I believe that Jean-Pierre has solved the mystery of how the Great Pyramid was built, and if the Egyptian government would let him, he could find the hidden ramps and perhaps more hidden chambers. Hopefully this will happen one day soon.

THE REVELATION

The Book of Revelation is a maze of symbols and archetypes that can be interpreted on both literal and symbolic levels. Much of the literal side of Revelation has been covered in our look at Old Testament prophecies, so in this chapter we will deal only with the symbolic interpretation.

The Revelation does not refer just to the Book of Revelation but to a revelation that will sweep the entire world at the beginning of the New Age. This new awareness is what the Book of Revelation deals with, and so this will be our starting point. Edgar Cayce gave a series of readings on The Revelation in which he related its symbolism to the human body. It is this understanding of the human body that will be the breakthrough in conventional religious thought that will lead us into the New Age.

This new understanding involves the seven endocrine glands of the body and is symbolized repeatedly in the Book of Revelation:

Chapter 1 — seven golden candlesticks,
seven churches, seven angels
Chapter 4 — seven lamps, seven seals
Chapter 8 — seven angels
Chapter 13 — seven heads

Chapter 15 — seven plagues

Chapter 17 — seven heads, seven mountains

All these "sevens" in Revelation are important to us. The Cayce readings tell us that these "sevens" symbolically represent the seven endocrine centers of the human body.

These endocrine centers are known to the Eastern religions as chakras. They are the pituitary, pineal, thyroid, thymus, adrenals, lyden, and the gonads. During meditation, energy known as kundalini is raised from the lyden and gonads through the nerve centers, up the spine to the brain, and finally to the pineal and pituitary glands.

It is this upward flow of energy that allows a person to get in touch with his or her spiritual self. Cayce links these seven glands with the seven churches mentioned in the Book of Revelation and with the colors associated with each of the glands:

1. Pituitary .... Violet—Laodicea—Highest Center
2. Pineal .... Indigo—Philadelphia—Third Eye
3. Thyroid .... Blue/Gray—Sardis—Will
4. Adrenals .... Yellow—Pergamos—Self-Preservation
6. Lyden .... Orange—Smyrna—Sustenance
7. Gonads .... Red—Ephesus—Propagation of Species

The existence of these seven glands fits with what is known as the Law of Octaves. In music you move up seven notes before moving to a new octave: do, re, mi, fa, so, la, ti, do. The same is true of the endocrine system. We must move upward through this system in order to move out of what we call our physical universe. The Law of Octaves is also demonstrated in nature by the fact that the genetic code, which transmits hereditary traits to offspring, contains 64 (8x8) bits of information.

We include it in our own systems in the 64 elements of the I Ching, 64 squares on a chess board, and the arrangement of all computers on a base 16 (2x8) system. The Law of Octaves is present in all levels of nature.

Jesus said, "Destroy this temple, and in three days I will raise it up." (John 2:19) He was referring to the temple of the body, which He raised three days after His crucifixion.

This is not the only human body symbolism in the Bible. In Revelation the beast rising out of the water symbolically represents the animal influences of the four lower centers: the thymus, adrenals, lyden, and gonads. In a similar vein, the sea of glass in Revelation 4:6 represents the calm emotions of John at the time of his vision. We meet the Father by calming our mind in meditation. This is symbolized by the sea of glass before the throne, the symbol for the brain. To complete the symbolism in chapter 5, the four and twenty elders represent the twenty-four cranial nerves of the brain's five senses.

Running between the seven endocrine centers and all the other centers in the body is the nervous system, referred to in the following section of Ecclesiastes as the "silver cord."

Ecclesiastes 12:5-7:
Also when they shall be afraid of that which is high, and fears shall be in the way, and the almond tree shall flourish, and the grasshopper shall be a burden, and the desire shall fail; because man goes to his long home, and the mourners go about the streets;

Or ever the silver cord is loosed or the golden bowl is broken, or the pitcher is broken at the fountain, or the wheel broken at the cistern;

Then shall the dust return to the earth as it was, and the spirit shall return to God, who gave it.

These verses are referring to the death of the body after the death of the nervous system. Electrical discharges produce a silver color, and the nervous system has a weak electrical current. So, this section of Ecclesiastes speaks of the human consciousness as contained within the nervous system. No doubt this is true, since everything we see, feel, smell, hear, and taste is associated with the nerves of the body.

These nerves are also closely associated with the seven endocrine centers. The seven glands affect the size of our bodies, our emotional and mental states, and just about everything else we are. Before we go any further, it would be useful for us to examine each of these centers and their effects individually.

1. **Gonads**. The sexual center is the most basic center of all, since it is involved with the production of our physical bodies. Just as protons and electrons came together in the beginning to form hydrogen, the first element, so male and female come together to form our physical bodies. Thus, this center is linked to the production of matter. As we will see, it is a very important point that the lower centers are linked to matter, and the higher centers are linked to energy. On the negative side the sex center provides lust, and on the positive side it provides opportunities for souls to enter the earth plane as newborn babies.

2. **Lyden.** There is not much information on the lyden. Cayce tells us it is involved with sustenance, or the absorption of food matter. It is the point in the passage of energy through the system.

3. **Adrenals.** The adrenals are the glands of fear. They give us that sudden rush of tension when we are in danger. For their size the adrenals have a very large blood supply, so that their secretions can get into the bloodstream in a hurry. Meaner and more combative animals have a wide adrenal cortex, while smaller, more timid animals have a narrow adrenal cortex. Humans have the widest adrenal cortex of all. As a lower center, the adrenals produce fear hormones, fear being one of the most destructive emotions of all. It is no coincidence that fear is associated with a lower center, while its opposite, faith, is associated with the higher centers.

4. **Thymus.** The thymus is called the gland of childhood because it is associated with our development at that stage. It stimulates the production of antibodies that protect the body from disease. The thymus is linked to the muscles and nutrition within our bodies. Cayce says that its emotion is love, and its location in the chest area may have something to do with the "heartache" we feel at times while in love.

5. **Thyroid.** The Cayce readings tell us that the thyroid is the gland of the will. This fits with what medical science tells us, since the thyroid controls the amount of energy used in the body. Its hormone, thyroxin, controls energy output. If a person applies his or her will, he or she can always find enough energy to accomplish a task. The thyroid is the pivotal point between the four lower centers and the two higher ones. The will controls which way the consciousness will go.

6. **Pineal.** René Descartes in his book, *Trait de L'Homme* in 1662, located the human soul in the pineal gland. Two thousand years ago the Hindus said the pineal was the "seat of the soul." Today, the pineal is often called the "third eye." This is

fascinating, since the cells in the pineal are almost identical to the cells in the retina of the eye. This may be why flashes of light are seen in higher states of consciousness. The mystical symbolism of the pineal is seen in the eye encased in the pyramid on the U.S. dollar bill. The pineal usually atrophies at age seven, which may be why Jesus said if we do not become "as little children," we cannot enter the kingdom of heaven. The pineal is the gateway to the highest center of all, the pituitary, since the pineal sits on the bundled nerves of the thalamus from which the pituitary hangs.

7. **Pituitary.** The pituitary is called the master gland by scientists because it controls all the other glands. It is about the size of an almond dangling from the end of a group of nerves known as the hypothalamus. The pituitary is so important to the body that removal will cause death in three days. It has its own skull, known as the Turkish saddle, which cradles it within our larger skull. Sexual development is one of the pituitary's functions, along with its more famous function of controlling the growth of the body. Underaction of the pituitary produces dwarfs; over action produces giants. Recent studies have shown that the pituitary produces natural painkillers known as endorphins. Western scientists have found that yogis trained in meditation can endure great physical pain by their production of endorphins. These endorphins may also be the cause of the "bliss" many people experience in meditation. Last, but not least, the pituitary controls the salt content of the body. The salt content of any liquid is directly related to its electrical conductivity. It is possible that this would explain why healers, such as Jesus, could produce power to heal. Certainly, this power also comes from higher levels, but at some point it must

manifest itself on this level. Electrical impulses may be one of these manifestations.

These are only a few of the capabilities of the pituitary. Dozens of hormones that it produces have been isolated, many of which are unknown in their function. Ultimately, we will discover that the pituitary is unlimited in its functions. In meditation it is the point at which we enter the holy of holies within ourselves.

In light of our study of the two higher glands it is important at this point to examine the involvement of the brain during meditation. The human brain has been compared to a "delicate flower perched on the end of a slender stalk." There are three sections in the brain called units. The third unit is concerned with planning and movement of the body. The second unit is concerned with the analysis of sensory input, e.g., seeing, hearing, etc. The first unit is the power supply. It is this unit that concerns us.

The *Encyclopedia of the Human Body* describes the first unit as follows:

"The first functional unit is located at the base of the brain and consists of the reticular formation, the midbrain, the thalamus, and the hypothalamus. It is the first area encountered by inputs from the sense organs and information stemming from the metabolic functions within the body. This unit plays a role in the regulation of activity in the cortex and maintains the alertness of the higher areas of the brain. It does this not by single isolated nerve impulses but by waves of electrical activity spreading throughout the unit and traveling up to the cortex. It is similar to a power source, which feeds the higher areas and which, if removed, causes a state of drowsiness."

The pituitary and pineal are connected to the first unit at the hypothalamus and thalamus. During meditation the third unit of the brain is "shut off" by sitting still and moving the body. The second unit is likewise shut off by clearing the mind of conscious thought. The only thing left is the first unit. As the quote indicates, waves of electrical energy flow up the spine to the thalamus, pineal, and the pituitary. This is the kundalini energy mentioned earlier. It is interesting to note that proper meditation requires calm emotions, and the thalamus, when diseased, produces fits of strong emotion. So the flow of energy in the thalamus is linked to the emotions, the sea of glass, mentioned in The Revelation by John.

All of this has been preached by mystics for thousands of years and is what Jesus meant when He said, "The kingdom of God is within you."

The Cayce readings have a great deal to say about the kundalini, as seen in the following readings:

Q. Are the following statements true or false? Comment on each as I read it: The life force rises

directly from the Leydig gland through the Gonads, thence to Pineal, and then to the other centers.

A. This is correct; though, to be sure, as it rises and is distributed through the other centers it returns to the solar plexus area for its impulse through the system.

For the moment, let's consider the variation here in this life force—or as respecting this life force. The question is asked not in relation to the life alone as manifested in the human body, but as to the process through which coordination is attained or gained in and through meditation, see? Hence, physically, as we

have indicated, there is first the nucleus—or the union of the first activities; and then the pineal as the long thread activity to the center of the brain, see? Then from there, as development progresses, there are those activities through reflexes to the growth or the developing of the body.

Interpret that variation, then, as being indicated here. One life force is the body-growth, as just described. The other is the impulse that arises, from the life center, in meditation. 281-53

Q. *How can I overcome the nerve strain I'm under at times?*

A. By closing the eyes and meditating from within, so that there arises—through that of the nerve system —that necessary element that makes along the PINEAL (Don't forget that this runs from the toes to the crown of the head!), that will quiet the whole nerve forces, making for that—as has been given—as the TRUE bread, the true strength of life itself. Quiet, meditation, for a half to a minute, will bring strength—[if the body will] see PHYSICALLY this flowing out to quiet self, whether walking, standing still, or resting. Well, too, that OFT, when alone MEDITATE in the silence—as the body HAS done. 311-4

These readings show us that the flow of energy involves not only meditation, but body growth as well. This agrees with what medical science has told us. This flow of energy must be directed to spiritual things or it can be harmful. If used in the spirit of love and for the good of all, it can become a great light as the following reading shows:

In the body we find that which connects the pineal, the pituitary, the lyden, may be truly called the silver cord, or the golden cup that may be filled with a closer walk with that which is the creative essence in physical, mental and spiritual life; for the destruction wholly of either will make for the disintegration of the soul from its house of clay. To be purely material minded, were an anatomical or pathological study made for a period of seven years (which is a cycle of change in all the body elements) of one that is acted upon through the third eye alone, we will find one fed upon spiritual things becomes a light that may shine from and in the darkest corner. One fed upon the purely material will become a Frankenstein that is without a concept of any influence other than material or mental. 262-20

In this reading Cayce mentions the "silver cord," as written about in Ecclesiastes, which may be "filled with a closer walk with . . . the creative essence" (God). It is interesting to note that Cayce says that one who acts through the third eye alone for seven years (the period it takes for every cell in the body to replace itself) would become a light to the world, while one fed only on the material world would become a Frankenstein monster! It is easy to think of examples of materially minded people in the world. But it is encouraging to note that all of us can develop spiritually in just seven years if we so desire.

Development through meditation involves not only the act of meditation itself but meditation with the highest possible purpose—in other words, being a channel of God's gifts to the people around you. What are these gifts? Love, patience, long-suffering, and forgiveness, to name just a few. With these purposes in mind meditation can become a most sublime and joyous experience.

I have been meditating for a number of years, so my experiences with meditation have been many and varied. Many times I have received guidance from the "still, small voice within." Usually, this guidance has been of great help to me. The only bad experience I can remember involved an insect that insisted on buzzing around my ear during my meditation. This buzzing was such a disturbance that the end of the meditation period found me exhausted from attempting to concentrate in an agitated frame of mind. The mind must be calm to properly meditate.

The rising of Kundalini energy in meditation can be experienced in a variety of ways. It can be seen as a series of waves spreading outward from a single point, then dissipating and starting over again. It spreads like ripples in a pond when you toss in a rock. Or, to put it another way, it looks like water poured on flat concrete which spreads out in a circle from a single point. It slowly flows into one's consciousness.

Another Kundalini experience is the bright light or, as some call it, "seeing the light." It comes as a light brighter than any light ever seen with the eyes, except that it is in the mind's eye. Once, when I was falling asleep, I was viewing an extremely bright sunset. I was in a meditative state inside a totally dark room. I reacted to the sunset by trying to close my eyes but found they were already closed! I have experienced this "light" several times since then, and it always occurs as an incredibly bright light between the eyes, the exact location of the pineal, the third eye.

The most vivid Kundalini energy I have ever experienced happened to me in a recent meditation session. I had been reading about raising energy up the spine and was attempting to do so just to see how much I could raise. This is not a good idea, because your purposes must be more pure than just having an "experience." As I was raising this energy, I visualized in my mind someone turning off a light. At the instant the light was turned off, I heard a loud audible snap! It sounded like a crackle of electricity or the snap of a bullwhip. At the same time I felt the energy flow that was going up my spine shut off with a sudden jolt. It was an unsettling experience that taught me that Kundalini is not something to be toyed with.

As the Cayce readings have said, this electrical energy is not just for the growth of the body. The readings go even further:

Thus there are the vibrations of the electrical energies of the body, for Life itself is electrical . . . 281-27

About fifty years ago, a Yale University neuroanatomist named Harold Burr found that there are electrical currents within all living organisms, from seeds to human beings.

He theorized that this electromagnetic field doesn't just reflect the electrical activity of the cells it envelops; it also controls and organizes them. Burr described it as "nature's Jello mold," shaping living matter just as a magnetic field patterns iron filings.

Magnifying all this is the fact that the brain is the most electrical organ in the body. Neurons account for only twenty percent of the brain's cells; the rest are mostly glial cells that sheathe the neurons. Evidence has been found that a direct current flows steadily through the glial cells.

Some scientists now believe that this direct current system, generally ignored by most brain researchers, may be the body's natural mechanism for cellular growth and repair. Science is gradually catching up with what the readings revealed many years ago.

This electrical current is very important to the theories we will look at next. The higher centers of the body are centers of energy, and the lower centers are more closely associated with matter. The importance of this can be understood when one has a grasp of Einstein's theory of relativity: As an object approaches the speed of light, time slows down. When said object reaches the speed of light, time stops.

In other words, at the speed of light time does not move. This part of Einstein's theory was proven in 1936 by Bell Laboratories. A radiating atom can act as a clock because it emits light at a definite frequency and wavelength in precise intervals. This can be measured by a spectroscope. Bell Labs compared the light given off by hydrogen atoms at high velocities with that of hydrogen atoms at rest. It was discovered that the frequency of vibration of the fast moving atoms slowed down in the exact manner Einstein had predicted. Another way of putting it would be that as the atoms speeded up, time slowed down.

Another example involves space travel. If a man left earth in a spaceship traveling at the speed of light, when he reached his destination he would be the same age as when he left. Even if several years had passed for people on the earth, our space traveler would not have aged at all. Even at the slow speeds automobiles and airplanes travel, time slows down, however slight the change may be. The change only becomes noticeable when speeds approach the speed of light, an incredible 186,000 miles per second.

All energy moves about the universe at the speed of light. So to energy and light, time is totally meaningless. Einstein put it as follows: "For us believing physicists time has the value of mere illusion, however tenacious." So time is an illusion belonging to the world of matter and not to the world of energy.

We know that consciousness operates through energy because the only thing that separates a dead body from a living body is electrical energy. The body without electricity is dead matter. At that point it exists only at the vibratory level of matter and not at the level from which our consciousness flows, which is energy.

The train of logic is as follows: The direct current flow of electricity in the human brain moves at 99.999% of the speed of light in the wake of our consciousness. Our consciousness exists at the level from which light and energy come, where time is stopped. If our consciousness exists where time is standing still, then our consciousness is eternal. Our brain acts as a brake to slow our consciousness down enough that it can operate at a level where the illusion of time does exist in our physical universe. This is the scientific proof that life is eternal.

This is why the higher centers of the body are associated with energy, and the lower centers of the body are associated with matter.

If you raise your consciousness in meditation, you connect with the energy level and your Eternal Being.

Until recently, this ramification of the theory of relativity was ignored, but now many people are beginning to look at the relationship among time, consciousness, and energy. Several books have been written on this subject, and in the future, discoveries in the world of physics will help awaken the world to the existence of eternal life.

The raising of consciousness to connect with the "eternal now" is the subject of the following Cayce reading:

As this life-force is expanded, it moves first from the Leydig center through the adrenals, in what may be termed an upward trend, to the pineal and to the centers in control of the emotions—or reflexes through the nerve forces of the body.

Thus an entity puts itself, through such an activity, into association or in conjunction with all it has EVER been or may be. For, it loosens the physical consciousness to the universal consciousness.

2475-1

Notice that Cayce says that moving upward to the pineal puts a person in contact with the past, present, and the future, the place where time does not move and all time is one. This is the universal consciousness or God.

Through this raising of energy we connect with God. This is nothing new. Mystics have been saying this for thousands of years, but now we know more about it through the realm of physics.

There are, of course, many connections between and light energy. The sun, the source of all life and light, is the most obvious connection. Jesus emitted a light or aura which Matthew says was as "white as snow." Eastern mystics talk about achieving "enlighten-ment," with the middle syllable being the word "light."

The Bible is full of references to light. Some are references to spiritual light, but there is more in their meaning. Paul saw a great light on the road to Damascus that changed him from persecuting the Christians to joining them. Here are just a few biblical references to light:

I John 1:5 "This then is the message which we have heard of him and declare to you, that God is light."

John 8:12 "I am the light of the world; he that follows me shall not walk in darkness, but shall have the light of life."

John 12:36 "While you have light, believe in the light, that you may be the Sons of Light."

Matthew 6:22 "The light of the body is the eye."

Light is often used as a symbol of spirituality, even to the point of saying, "God is Light." Jesus referred to himself as the "light of the world" and to the light of the body as the "eye" or the third eye. Thus,

Jesus has shown that the energy flow to the third eye is the spiritual light of the human body. This is the most important point in these references, because it shows the way of development for all of us.

In one of his readings. Cayce described the use of light appearing in a six-sided crystal as a "means of communication between infinite and the finite." (2072-10) Since the source of light itself is the infinite, it would make sense that one could communicate with the "infinite" in this way.

One of the Cayce readings we looked at earlier referred to Jesus returning and receiving as many as had "quickened" themselves through living a spiritual life. All of the universe, matter and energy, is made up of vibrations. Energy is a quicker vibration than matter. The use of meditation and spiritual living quickens the body of matter to the level of energy, and beyond to the universal consciousness. "Quickening" is a perfect description of an increase in the frequency of vibrations, that is, a shift from matter to energy.

The raising of consciousness is central to the future: first, because the raising of vibrations among the human race is what will attract Jesus to return; second, because if one gets in touch with his or her eternal spirit, then physical death has no power. If earth changes occur, many people will die. But if they have quickened themselves, their spirits will live on and reincarnate during the millennium. So those who quicken themselves will survive, even if they die.

Many books about the end times speak of survival in terms of storing food and such, but true survival is based on the growth of a person's soul. This is the message of Jesus' death and resurrection.

The idea of light and the raising of consciousness is relevant to the prophecies for a number of other reasons. It represents the change that will occur in religious thought throughout the world. People will develop themselves through meditation, and science will come to recognize this development. Particularly, the science of physics will lead the way in the field of understanding consciousness.

This understanding of consciousness includes much more than just the consciousness of humanity. Physics is moving toward understanding the universe and universal consciousness, an idea that has been held by Eastern religions for many years. The universe has been described as a thought in the mind of God, and now physicists are saying that the universe behaves more like "a great thought than a machine."

One of the most important theories developed in physics in the last few years is called Bell's theorem. In a series of very complicated mathematical proofs, physicist J.S. Bell has shown that everything in the universe is connected to everything else, even though they may be separated by great distances. In other words, everything is part of one thing, i.e., God, the Creative Force, etc.

There is evidence for this in other scientific truths. German physicist Max Planck proved that all energy radiations were a function of one number, now known as "Planck's constant." If all energy is a function of one number, then surely all energy is a function of one thing. This one thing is the Creative Force or God.

Einstein proved that energy and matter were essentially equivalent or were different vibratory levels of the same thing. Energy and matter are part of one force or, as the Bible says, "The Lord thy God is One." This can be shown mathematically with Einstein's famous equivalence equation:

$$E=mc2$$

Divide both sides by E...

$$\frac{E}{E} = \frac{mc^2}{E} \qquad 1 = \frac{mc^2}{E}$$

The information we have just looked at proves that the universe is a part of one whole. This whole is both physical and nonphysical. Physical things exist in the third dimension, but the universe was created from the fourth dimension, the dimension of consciousness. Time is not the fourth dimension as many believe; thought, ideas, consciousness are the fourth dimension. Before anything exists in the physical universe, it must first be an idea. Before a bridge is built, someone must think of the idea of building it. The same is true of the creation of the universe. God conceived of the universe first, and it was created. The point here is that the three-dimensional One we are part of is only part of the universal consciousness. Three-dimensional reality is only a shadow of spiritual reality. Everything in reality follows the same pattern: fourth-dimensional idea—creative action—third-dimensional reality. This is the way our three-dimensional universe was created and is still being created today.

THE FIFTH ROOT RACE

While discussing how the Hall of Records might be found, Edgar Cayce gave the following information:

This may not be entered without an understanding, for those that were left as guards may NOT be passed until after a period of their regeneration in the Mount, or the fifth root race begins. 5748-6

Cayce tells us that the Hall of Records may not be entered until "the fifth root race begins." The question of course is, "What is a fifth root race?" A root race is not a race like we normally think of in terms of black, white, yellow, brown, or red. The term "root race" refers to the human race or, as the scientists refer to it, *Homo sapiens*.

The idea of root races is well established in mystical tradition. The nineteenth-century mystic, Madam Blavatsky, referred to seven or more root races as preceding *Homo sapiens*. Cayce tells us that there were four previous root races, but as is often the case with the Cayce readings, no one asked Mr. Cayce what those four root races were. However, from my forty years of study of the Cayce readings, I believe the four root races were spirit, thought form, projection into matter, and, finally, Adamic human, or *Homo sapiens*.

The Cayce readings tell us that there is going to be a new physical type of human being, which will begin around the time that the Hall of Records is opened in Egypt.

In order to get a better understanding of what all this means, I think it would be valuable for us to look back at Cayce's story of the history of humankind.

Cayce tells us that humans did not evolve from the apes. Cayce says that the souls were originally in the Spirit, and that there was a "rebellion in the celestial," and the souls began to project themselves into matter and became separated from God. He says that they could project themselves at will into matter, be it trees, rocks, animals, whatever. He says the souls "became the things that the minerals were."

Gradually, they took on a form that was denser than spirit, and Cayce called this form the "thought form." This makes sense since a mental form is more concentrated than pure Spirit. These thought forms had the ability to take shape in thought, "much in the way and manner as the amoeba would in the waters of a stagnant bay, or lake, in the present" (364-3).

These thought forms projected into matter, and their bodies hardened such that they became trapped in matter. Some souls became so trapped that they were little more than automatons, and Cayce called these creatures the "things." They were brut like creatures, and they took on many different forms such as giants and dwarfs. Genesis 6:4 tells us that "there were giants in the earth in those days . . ." Interestingly enough, this aspect of Cayce's creation story is confirmed by anthropologists. Fossils have been discovered of giant humanoids such as Gigantopithecus, a human ancestor that stood over eight feet tall and weighed 400 to 500 pounds. In addition fossils of dwarflike human ancestors such as Australopithecus have also been discovered.

After the souls became trapped in matter, other souls came into the earth to help—not by their own will, but by the will of God. Cayce called these souls, "the sons of god." The sons of god were androgynous, with both sexes being contained in one body:

In the beginning, as was outlined, there was presented that that became as the Sons of God, in that male and female were as one, with those abilities for those changes as were able or capable of being brought about. 364-7

The sons of god had tremendous occult powers, but they, too, became entangled in matter and began to separate into male and female. Genesis 6:2 says that "the sons of God saw the daughters of men that they were fair; and they took them wives of all whom they chose." This is a poetic description of the separating of the Sons of God into male and female.

At this point there were many different forms on the earth. There were the things, the thought forms, the sons of god, giants, dwarfs, etc. A group of the sons of god led by one named Amilius realized that things were out of control, and one form needed to be created to accommodate all the different souls. So Amilius and the sons of god created Adamic human or *Homo sapiens.* Cayce constantly quotes Job 38:7 in this regard:

"Where were you when I laid the foundations of the earth? When the morning stars sang together, and all the sons of God shouted for joy?"

Cayce tells us that the five races were projected into five different places simultaneously. The skin color of each race matching the soil where the projection took place. The white, the Caucasus;

the black, Africa; the brown, India; the yellow, the Gobi; and the red, Atlantis.

Cayce's description of a simultaneous projection of *Homo sapiens* fits well with what anthropologists say happened to early humans. They tell us that about 33,000 B.C. *Homo sapiens* sprang forth and many of the older forms of humanoids became extinct. Scientists call this period the "Great Leap Forward." They call it this because during this period human culture became more sophisticated overnight. Sophisticated tools such as fishing hooks and bows and arrows appeared. Primitive art such as cave paintings became more sophisticated, as well. In Europe during this period the relatively primitive Neanderthal man became extinct, and *Homo sapiens*, or Adamic human, became the dominant form.

How was the Adamic human created? This was never fully explained in the Cayce readings, but one reading uses the term "introgression" (5748-6) to describe the process. The word "introgression" means gene splicing. This is fascinating since scientists tell us that the difference between primitive human and modern human is a one percent change in our genetic material, DNA.

All of this leads us up to today, and the question, how is modern human is going to make this physical change to the fifth root race?

The only way that humans can change physically is by a change in their genetic code, DNA. But how does one's genetic code change? I see three distinct possibilities as agents of this change.

The first possibility is that we will change our own genetic code scientifically. Scientists are already doing this through gene splicing. They have learned how to change our genetic code by taking out DNA from our genes and replacing it with different DNA.

In this way they have learned how to cure certain types of genetic defects in children. If a child has a defective gene that prevents his or her body from performing its proper function, scientists can now replace that gene with a non-defective gene so that the body will perform normally.

Other amazing things have been done with animals and plants. Recombinant DNA research has created mice with human lungs that help scientists do medical research. They have also combined a goat and a sheep to create a creature they call a "geep." They are currently working on making tomatoes that ripen at the grocery store, and vegetables that stay ripe for very long periods of time without refrigeration.

We have mapped the human genome and other species as well. This opens up tremendous possibilities. Besides curing genetic diseases, scientists might discover genes for mathematical ability, musical ability, and athletic ability that they could genetically engineer into a person's body. There is also the possibility that genes will be discovered that will slow or reverse the aging process. Scientists have already been able to double the life span of certain animals through genetic engineering. They may be able to create a completely new type of human being—the fifth root race that Cayce talks about.

The second possible cause for a change in our genetic code involves the predicted earth changes. There may be a shift in the earth's magnetic poles, which scientists tell us periodically reverse themselves. When the earth's magnetic poles reverse themselves, the earth's magnetic field drops to zero. The earth's magnetic field is the only thing that protects the earth from exposure to cosmic radiation. By studying past magnetic field reversals and fossil records, scientists have discovered that when the earth's magnetic field reverses, old forms of life die and new ones appear. Scientists theorize that this is because exposure to cosmic radiation can cause genetic mutations. So the predicted pole shift could expose people on the earth to cosmic radiation that could cause them to change genetically into another form. As I mentioned earlier scientists believe we are currently in the beginning of a magnetic field reversal.

The third possible agent of change that could create a fifth root race is what I call the supernatural event. This involves the direct intervention of angelic forces on the earth. This seems to be the way that *Homo sapiens*, or the fourth root race, was created. Cayce says that the five races were projected to five places simultaneously by the sons of god. The same kind of thing could occur again. There is evidence for this in the Cayce readings and the Bible:

1 Corinthians 15:51-52
Behold, I show you a mystery: We shall not all sleep, but we shall all be changed. In a moment, in the twinkling of an eye, at the last trumpet; for the trumpet shall sound, and the dead shall be raised incorruptible, and we shall be changed.

These verses from Corinthians tell us that "we shall all be changed." Could this refer to the change of the human body to the fifth root race? I think it could. This passage also gives us the time frame for this event. It says that this will occur "at the last trumpet." In Matthew 24 Jesus tells us that the last trumpet will be sounded with his return to earth. So I believe the fifth root race will begin with the return of Jesus.

Cayce himself was asked about the meaning of this section of 1 Corinthians. This is what he said:

Q. Please explain 1 Cor. 15:51. Is the reference here to the body? "Behold, I show you a mystery. We shall not all sleep, but we shall all be changed."

A. Referring to the body; though the individual here speaking (Paul) LOOKED for this to happen in his own day, see? 262-87

Cayce tells us that this passage of Corinthians refers to the body. Then he goes on to say that Paul expected this change to happen in his own day, thus implying that this change will happen in the future. That is what I think will happen.

There are other passages in the Bible that refer to this event:

1 Thessalonians 4:16-17

For the Lord himself shall descend from heaven with a shout, with the voice of the archangel, and with the trumpet of God; and the dead in Christ shall rise first.

Then we who are alive and remain shall be caught up together with them in the clouds, to meet the Lord in the air; and so shall we ever be with the Lord.

Once again, we see that the trumpet is mentioned in the description of the return of Jesus. This is the "Lord himself shalt descend from heaven with a shout" verse. In another parallel with 1 Corinthians, 1 Thessalonians says that the "dead in Christ shall rise first." Finally, there is a reference to those "who are alive" being "caught up together with them in the clouds." So something will happen to those people who are alive. I believe this "something" will be the creation of the new root race Cayce talks about.

Cayce echoes 1 Thessalonians in the following reading:

He will not tarry, for having overcome He shall appear even AS the Lord AND Master. Not as one born, but as one that returneth to His own, for He will walk and talk with men of every clime, and those that are faithful and just in their reckoning shall be caught

up with Him to rule and to do JUDGMENT for a thousand years! 364-7

Cayce discusses the return of Jesus as one who "will walk and talk with men of every clime." He then goes on to quote 1 Thessalonians when he says that those who are "faithful and just in their reckoning shall be caught up with Him to rule and to do JUDGMENT for a thousand years!" "Caught up" definitely implies some sort of change for the people involved.

Other readings also seem to imply this change.

As to times, as to seasons, as to places, ALONE is it given to those who have named the name—and who bear the mark of those of His calling and His election in their bodies. To them it shall be given. 3976-15

This reading talks about those "who bear the mark of those of His calling and His election in their bodies." Now that's a curious phrase. Not those who bear the mark of His calling in their hearts or minds or souls but in their bodies. This could be a reference to the change of our bodies to a new root race.

The following reading also seems to imply a change in us with Jesus' return.

So, as He [Jesus] gave, "I leave thee, but I will come again and receive as many as ye have quickened through the manifesting in thy life the will of the Father in the earth." 262-58

Jesus will come again and receive those who have "quickened."

All of these quotes from the Bible and the Cayce readings refer to some kind of action. We shall all be "changed," we shall be "caught up," we shall be "quickened." I believe all these references refer to the creation of the fifth root race.

What will this new root race be like? We don't really know. We do know that it will be more evolved than we are at the present. Perhaps we will be like the sons of god with androgynous bodies and occult powers. Perhaps we will have energy bodies. We may evolve into something totally different than we have ever seen before. There is no way to tell for sure.

ANGELS OR ALIENS

Given all that we have learned so far, I want to talk about the role our alien friends may have in the fulfillment of the prophecies. I want to start by going through a brief history of UFOs, and then looking at what they are doing, and why they are here.

The Battle of Los Angeles

The Battle of Los Angeles is the name given to an alleged attack on Los Angeles by unknown flying objects on Feb 25, 1942. The U.S. military believed that Japanese planes were attacking the West Coast when an unknown flying object was picked up on radar over the city in the early morning hours. Initially, the target of the aerial barrage was thought to be an attacking force from Japan, but speaking at a press conference shortly afterward, Secretary of the Navy Frank Knox called the incident a "false alarm."

But a photo from the Los Angeles Times the next day shows a UFO caught in the searchlights with anti-aircraft shells exploding all around it. The Office of Air Force history describes the attack as follows:

During the night of 24/25 February 1942, unidentified objects caused a succession of alerts in southern California. On the 24th, a warning issued by naval intelligence indicated that an attack

could be expected within the next ten hours. That evening a large number of flares and blinking lights were reported from the vicinity of defense plants. An alert called at 1918 [7:18 p.m., Pacific time] was lifted at 2223, and the tension temporarily relaxed. But early in the morning of the 25th renewed activity began. Radars picked up an unidentified target 120 miles west of Los Angeles. Antiaircraft batteries were alerted at 0215 and were put on Green Alert—ready to fire—a few minutes later. The AAF kept its pursuit planes on the ground, preferring to await indications of the scale and direction of any attack before committing its limited fighter force. Radars tracked the approaching target to within a few miles of the coast, and at 0221 the regional controller ordered a blackout. Thereafter the information center was flooded with reports of "enemy planes," even though the mysterious object tracked in from sea seems to have vanished. At 0243, planes were reported near Long Beach, and a few minutes later a coast artillery colonel spotted "about 25 planes at 12,000 feet" over Los Angeles. At 0306 a balloon carrying a red flare was seen over Santa Monica and four batteries of anti-aircraft artillery opened fire, whereupon "the air over Los Angeles erupted like a volcano." From this point on reports were hopelessly at variance.

The object was first tracked 120 miles west of Los Angeles which would be out over the Pacific Ocean. Then it mysteriously vanished. Next a "balloon with a red flare" was seen over Santa Monica. 14,000 shells were fired at the object, yet no wreckage was found. Indeed, a retired college professor reported seeing the object float down the coast and back out to sea. He described it as silver in color.

Reports from the Los Angeles Times the next day:

"Air Raid! Come here quick! Look over there, those searchlights. They've got something. They're blasting it with anti-aircraft!" Father, mother, children all gathered on the front porch, congregated in small clusters in the blackout streets -- against orders. Babies cried, dogs barked, doors slammed. But the objects in the sky slowly moved on, caught in the center of the lights like the hub of a bicycle wheel surrounded by gleaming spokes.

And from a national wire report:

Anti-aircraft guns fired round after round of ammunition and tracer bullets at an unidentified object which moved slowly down the coast from Santa Monica and disappeared south of the rich Signal Hill oil fields early today.

Army officials declined to comment, but speculation quickly arose that an enemy blimp might have passed over the area. This was based on the fact the object required nearly 30 minutes to travel some 20 or 25 miles -- far slower than an airplane.

After the shelling stopped, shrapnel rained down on the city for an hour and several people were killed. Then the first UFO cover up in history began. From the Office of Air Force history:

Attempts to arrive at an explanation of the incident quickly became as involved and mysterious as the "battle" itself. The Navy immediately insisted that there was no evidence of the presence of enemy planes, and [Secretary of the Navy], Frank Knox announced at a press conference on 25 February that the raid was just a false alarm. At the same conference he admitted that attacks were always possible and indicated that vital industries located along the coast ought to be moved inland. The Army had a hard time making up its mind on the cause of the alert. A report to Washington, made by the Western Defense Command shortly after the raid had ended, indicated that the credibility of reports of an attack had begun to be shaken before the blackout was lifted. This message predicted that developments would prove "that most previous reports had been greatly exaggerated." The Fourth Air Force had indicated its belief that there were no planes over Los Angeles. But the Army did not publish these initial conclusions. Instead, it waited a day, until after a thorough examination of witnesses had been finished. On the basis of these hearings, local commanders altered their verdict and indicated a belief that from one to five unidentified airplanes had been over Los Angeles. Secretary Stimson announced this conclusion as the War Department version of the incident, and he advanced two theories to account for the mysterious craft: either they were commercial planes operated by an enemy from secret fields in California or Mexico, or they were light planes launched from Japanese submarines. In either case, the enemy's purpose must have been to locate anti-aircraft defenses in the area or to deliver a blow at civilian morale.

The military had no explanation of what the craft were, and after the war the Japanese said they had no submarines or aircraft in the area. Clearly the photograph from the Los Angeles Times shows a classic flying saucer outline, which would make one think that the craft was extraterrestrial. That plus the fact that 14,000 anti-aircraft shells fired at it could not bring it down.

UFOs over Washington

On July 19, 1952 radar operators at the Washington DC airport spotted several UFO on their scopes over the Capitol Building and the White House. Other radar sites were notified and jets were scrambled. When the jets arrived on the scene, the UFOs disappeared. When the jets left, the UFOs reappeared. At 530 am in the morning the UFOS disappeared from the radar scopes entirely. Witnesses reported seeing orange balls of light and huge disks flying in formation.

One week later on July 26th more UFOs appeared over DC. They were seen by airline pilots and tracked on radar from several locations. Their speeds varied from slow to 7,000 mph. Once again jets were scrambled. One of the fighters spotted four UFOs and gave chase, at which point the UFOs changed direction and surrounded the fighter. Then they took off at impossible speeds.

The publicity from the two weekends of sighting was so great that the Air Force held a press conference on July 29th in which General John Samford declared that the UFOs were stars, meteors, and temperature inversions and posed no credible threat the United States.

The main desire on the part of the Air Force at this point was to get the public off their back, and the press conference succeeded. This was the beginning of a history of Air Force attempts to downplay any UFO sightings in order to keep any information that might be gained from such sightings a non-story.

Westall Australia UFO
On April 6, 1966 a UFO flew over Westall High School in Melbourne, Australia. Hundreds of students were outside at the time, as the saucer-shaped UFO landed in a park behind the school. It then took off and was seen and photographed by one of the teachers with a 35mm camera.

A couple of hours after the landing the military arrived at the school and literally wrestled the camera and film away from the teacher and told the students not to discuss the landing with anyone including the press. Fortunately some students ignored the warning and spoke to the newspapers. Otherwise, the story might have died.

UFOs interest in nuclear bases

During the 1960's, 1970's, and 1980's UFOs took a particular interest in American nuclear bases and even made several incursions into nuclear weapons storage areas. On March 16, 1967, they visited Malmstrom AFB in Great Falls, Montana and shut down ten nuclear missiles.

The following story is as told by Robert Salas who was the DMCCC in O-Flight that morning:

My recollection is that I was on duty as a Deputy Missile Combat Crew Commander below ground in the LCC, during the morning hours of 16 March 1967.

Outside, above the subterranean LCC capsule, it was a typical clear, cold Montana night sky; there were a few inches of snow on the ground. Where we were, there were no city lights to detract from the spectacular array of stars, and it was not uncommon to see shooting stars. Montana isn't called "Big Sky Country" for no reason, and Airmen on duty topside probably spent some of their time outside looking up at the stars. It was one of those airmen who first saw what at first appeared to be a star begin to zig-zag across the sky. Then he saw another light do the same thing, and this time it was larger and closer. He asked his Flight Security Controller, (FSC, the Non-Commissioned Officer (NCO) in charge of Launch Control Center site security), to come and take a look. They both stood there watching the lights streak directly

above them, stop, change directions at high speed and return overhead. The NCO ran into the building and phoned me at my station in the underground capsule. He reported to me that they had been seeing lights making strange maneuvers over the facility, and that they weren't aircraft. I replied: "Great. You just keep watching them and let me know if they get any closer."

I did not take this report seriously and directed him to report back if anything more significant happened. At the time, I believed this first call to be a joke. Still, that sort of behavior was definitely out of character for air security policemen whose communications with us were usually very professional.

A few minutes later, the security NCO called again. This time he was clearly frightened and was shouting his words:

"Sir, there's one hovering outside the front gate!"

"One what?"

"A UFO! It's just sitting there. We're all just looking at it. What do you want us to do?"

"What? What does it look like?"

"I can't really describe it. It's glowing red. What are we supposed to do?"

"Make sure the site is secure and I'll phone the Command Post."

"Sir, I have to go now, one of the guys just got injured."

Before I could ask about the injury, he was off the line. I immediately went over to my commander, Lt. Fred Meiwald, who was on a scheduled sleep period. I woke him and began to brief him about the phone calls and what was going on topside. In the middle of this conversation, we both heard the first alarm klaxon resound through the confined space of the capsule, and both immediately looked over at the panel of annunciator lights at the Commander's station. A 'No-Go' light and two red security lights were lit indicating problems at one of our missile sites. Fred jumped up to query the system to determine the cause of the problem. Before he could do so, another alarm went off at another site, then another and another simultaneously. Within the next few seconds, we had lost six to eight missiles to a 'No-Go' (inoperable) condition.

After reporting this incident to the Command Post, I phoned my security guard. He said that the man who had approached the UFO had not been injured seriously but was being evacuated by helicopter to the base. Once topside, I spoke directly with the security guard about the UFOs. He added that the UFO had a red glow and appeared to be saucer shaped. He repeated that it had been immediately outside the front gate, hovering silently.

We sent a security patrol to check our LFs after the shutdown, and they reported sighting another UFO during that patrol. They also lost radio contact with our site immediately after reporting the UFO.

When we were relieved by our scheduled replacement crew later that morning. The missiles had still not been brought on line by on-site maintenance teams.

None of the ten missiles that were shut down were connected to each other in any way, and some were miles apart.

October-November 1975

During the fall of 1975 American Air Force bases all along the Canadian border were visited by UFOs. Loring AFB in Maine,

Wurtsmith AFB in Michigan, and Malmstrom AFB in Montana all had UFOs or "helicopters" visit them. The following descriptions were all contained in official Department of Defense documents obtained by the Freedom of Information Act as well as in the fine book, Clear Intent: The Government Coverup of the Ufo Experience Paperback 1984 by Lawrence Fawcett and Barry J. Greenwood. I cannot emphasis enough that these are official Air Force documents. At first they call the UFOS "helicopters" but after a few nights of these UFO visits, the Air Force just gave up and started calling them UFOs. Keep in mind the following passages are direct quotes from official United States Air Force documents:

DEPARTMENT OF THE AIR FORCE HEADQUARTERS
AEROSPACE DEFENSE COMMAND PETERSON AIR FORCE
BASE. COLORADO 80914
Request for Information Under the Freedom of Information Act

NORAD Command Director's Log (1975).

29 October/0630Z: Command Director called by Air Force Operations Center concerning an unknown heli-copter landing in the munitions storage area at Loring AFB, Maine. Apparently this was second night in a row for this occurrence. There was also an indication, but not continued, that Canadian bases had been over-flown by a helicopter.

31 October/0445Z: Report from Wurtsmith AFB through Air Force Ops Center - incident at 0355Z. Helicopter hovered over SAC weapons storage area then departed area. Tanker flying at 2700 feet Made both visual sighting and radar skin Oaint. Tracked object 35NM SE over Lake Huron where contact was lost.

1 November/0920Z: Received, as info, message from Loring AFB, Maine, citing probable helicopter overflight of base.

8 November/0753Z: 24th NORAD Region unknown track J330, heading -- SSW, 12000 feet. 1 to 7 objects, 46.46N 109.23W. Two F-106 scrambled out of Great Falls at 0745Z. SAC reported visual sighting from Sabotage Alert Teams (SAT) Kl, K3, LI and L6 (lights and jet sounds). Weather section states no anomalous propagation or northern lights. 0835Z SAC SAT Teams K3 and L4 report visual, K3 reports target at 300 feet altitude and L4 reports target at 5 miles. Contact lost at 08202. F-106s returned to base at 0850Z with negative results. 0905Z Great Falls radar search and height had intermittent contact. 0910Z SAC teams again had visual (Site C-1, 10 miles SE Stanford, Montana). 0920Z SAC CP reported that when F-106s were in area, targets would turn out lights, and when F-106s left, targets would turn lights one F-106s never gained visual or radar contact at any time due to terrain clearance. This same type of activity has been reported in the Malmstrom area for several days although previous to tonight no unknowns were declared. The track will be carried as a remaining unknown.

b. 24th NCB Region Senior Director's Log (Malmstrom AFB, Montana).

7 Nov 75 (1035Z) - Received a call from the 341st Strategic Air Command Post (SAC CP), saying that the following missile locations reported seeing a large red to orange to yellow object: M-1, L-3, LIMA and L-6. The general object location would be 10 miles south of Moore, Montana, and 20 miles east of Buffalo, Montana. Commander and Deputy for Operations (DO) info/med.

7 Nov 75 (1203z) - SAC advised that the LCF at. Harlowton, Montana, observed an object which emitted a light which illuminated the site driveway. 7 Nov 75 (1319Z) - SAC advised K®1 says very bright object to their east is now southeast of them and they are looking at it with 10x50 binoculars. Object seems to have lights (several) on it, but no distinct pattern. The orange/gold

object overhead also has small lights on it. SAC also advises female civilian reports having seen an object bearing south from her position six miles west of Lewistown.

7 Nov 75 (1327Z) - L-1 reports that the object to their northeast seems to be issuing a black object from it, tubular in shape. In all this time, surveillance has not been able to detect any sort of track except for known traffic. 7 Nov 75 (1355Z) - K-1 and L-1 report that as the sun rises, so do the objects they have visual.

7 Nov 75 (1429Z) - From SAC CP: As the sun. rose, the UFOs disappeared. Commander and DO notified.

8 Nov 75 (0635Z) - A security caAper team at K-4 reported UFO with white lights. one red light 50 yards behind white light. Personnel at K-1 seeing same object.

8 Nov 75 (0645Z) - Height personnel picked up objects 10-13,000 feet, Track J330, EKLB 0648, 18 knots, 9,500 feet. Objects as many as seven, as few as two A/C.

8 Nov 75 (0753Z) - J330 unknown 0753. Stationary/seven knots/ 12,000. One (varies seven objects). None, no possibility, EKLB 3746, two F-106, GTF, SCR 0754. NCOC notified.

8 Nov 75 (0820Z) - Lost radar contact, fighters broken off at 0825, looking in area of J331 (another height finder contact). 8 Nov 75 (0905Z) - From SAC CP; L-sites had fighters and objects; fighters did not get down to objects.

8 Nov 75 (0915Z) - Prom SAC CP From four different points Observed objects and fighters; when fighters arrived in the area, the lights went out; when fighters departed, the lights came back on; to NCOC.

8 Nov 75 (0953Z) From SAC CP: L-5 reported object increased in speed - high velocity, raised in altitude and now cannot tell the object from stars. To NCOC.

8 Nov 75 (1105Z) - From SAC CPt E-1 reported a bright white light (site is approximately 60 nautical miles north of Lewistown). NCOC notified.

—9 Nov 75 (0305Z) * SAC CP called and advised SAC crews at Sites L-1, L-6 and M-1 observing UFO. Object yellowish bright round light 20 miles north of Harlowton, 2 to 4,000 feet.

-- 9 Nov 75 (0320Z) - SAC CP reports UFO 20 miles southeast of Lewistown, orange white disc object. 24th NORLD Region surveilletnc-checking area. Surveillance unable to get height check.

--9 Nov 75 (0320Z) - FAA Watch Supervisor reported he had five air carriers vicinity of UFO, United Flight 157 reported seeing meteor, "arc welder's blue" in color. SAC CP advised, sites still report seeing object stationary.

9 Nov 75 (0348Z) - SAC CP confirms L-I, sees oblect, a mobi/4), security team has been directed to get closer and report.

9 Nov 75 (0629Z) - SAC CP advises UFO sighting reported around 0305Z. Cancelled the flight security team from Site 1,-1, checked area and all secure, no more sightings.

10 Nov 75 (0215Z) - Received a call from SAC CP. Report UFO sighting from site K-1 around Harlowton area. Surveillance checking area with height finder.

10 Nov 75 (0153Z) - Surveillance report unable to locate track that would correlate with UFO sighted by K-1.

10 Nov 75 (1125Z) - UFO sighting reported by Minot Air Force Station, a bright star-like object in the west, moving east, about the size of a car. First seen approximately 1015Z. Approximately 1120Z, the object passed over the radar station, 1,000 feet to 2,000 feet high, no noise heard. Three people from the site or local area saw the object.

So UFOs were penetrating American Air Force bases and hovering over nuclear storage areas. Why? Was to intimidate the U.S. government into cooperating? Was it to keep us from destroying ourselves? Were they merely curious?

The Rendlesham Forest Incident

In December of 1980, RAF Woodbridge, an air base in England that was being used by the U.S. Air Force, was visited over a three day period by a series of UFOs. Initially security personal saw what they thought was a plane crash into the Rendlesham Forest. When they went to investigate they saw UFOs moving through the trees. Jim Penniston, a security guard, claims to have encountered a triangular craft, covered in hieroglyphic-like characters. "I estimated it to be about three metres tall and about three metres wide at the base," Penniston later explained. "No landing gear was apparent, but it seemed like she was on fixed legs. I moved a little closer. I had already taken all 36 pictures on my roll of film. I walked around the craft, and finally, I walked right up to the craft. I noticed the fabric of the shell was more like a smooth, opaque, black glass." Penniston made drawings of the craft in his notebook which are quite amazing.

Indentations on the forest floor, as well as damage to the trees in the area where the lights had been spotted, were found the following morning. Radiation levels recorded at the site of the indentations were much higher than normal.

Two nights later, a different set of military personnel led by Lieutenant Colonel Charles Halt experienced a similar series of events. Halt intended to disprove the wild rumors swirling around RAF bases Woodbridge and Bentwaters. Arming himself with a tape recorder, he set out to investigate. The subsequent audio tape is now considered one of the most valuable pieces of evidence in the Rendlesham Forest incident.

The transcript of the tape runs to some 18 minutes but includes statements from Halt such as: "I see it too... it's back again... it's coming this way... there's no doubt about it... this is weird... it looks like an eye winking at you... it almost burns your eyes... he's coming toward us now... now we're observing what appears to be a beam coming down to the ground... one object still hovering over Woodbridge base... beaming down". Halt has since given interviews in which he claims that these occurrences were picked up by British radar. "I didn't know this until recently," he told AOL News. "Because people have come forward after they've retired. There were two radar confirmations."

After it was over, Colonel Halt wrote a memo about the event that was eventually leaked to the press.

The Belgium UFO Wave

The Belgian UFO wave began on November 29, 1989. A large triangular UFO was seen by no less than thirty different groups of witnesses, and three separate groups of police officers. The craft was of a flat, triangular shape, with lights underneath. This giant craft did not make a sound as it slowly moved across the landscape of Belgium. There was free sharing of information as the Belgian populace tracked this craft as it moved from the town of Liege to the border of the Netherlands and Germany. One policeman said, "It was beautiful, and I knew then that we were not alone in the universe."

The Belgian UFO wave peaked with the events of the night of 30/31 March 1990. On that night unknown objects were tracked on radar, chased by two Belgian Air Force F-16s, photographed, and were sighted by an estimated 13,500 people on the ground – 2,600 of whom filed written statements describing in detail what they had seen. Following the incident the Belgian air force released a report detailing the events of that night including radar data.

The Phoenix Lights

On March 13, 1997 a giant boomerang shaped craft flew over the city of Phoenix, Arizona for over an hour. Hundreds of witnesses saw it, and some reported that it was "bigger than an aircraft carrier," and that "if you held up a newspaper, you could not cover the sight of this craft."

Tim Ley and his wife Bobbi, his son Hal and his grandson Damien Turnidge saw the craft. At first they appeared to them as five separate and distinct lights in an arc-shape like they were on top of a balloon, but they soon realized the lights appeared to be moving towards them. Over the next ten or so minutes they appeared to be coming closer and the distance between the lights increased and they took on the shape of an upside down V. Eventually when the lights appeared to be a couple of miles away the witnesses could make out a shape that looked like a 60-degree carpenter's square with the five lights set into it, with one at the front and two on each side. Soon the object with the embedded lights appeared to be coming right down the street where they lived about 100 to 150 feet above them, traveling so slowly it appeared to hover and was silent. The object then seemed to pass over their heads and went through a V opening in the peaks of the mountain range towards Squaw Peak Mountain. Researchers estimated that the craft was 1,400 feet wide.

Arizona Governor Fife Symington originally made fun of the event, but then later said that he had also witnessed the "crafts of unknown origin" during the 1997 event, although he did not go public with the information. In an interview with The Daily Courier in Prescott Arizona, Symington said, "I'm a pilot and I know just about every machine that flies. It was bigger than anything that I've ever seen. It remains a great mystery. Other people saw it, responsible people. I don't know why people would ridicule it".

Illinois UFO

On January 5, 2000 a UFO traveled over the towns of Highland, Dupo, Lebanon, Summerfield, Millstadt, and O'Fallon. Five on-duty Illinois police officers in separate locales, along with various other witnesses, reported the massive, silent, triangular aircraft operating at an unusual range of near-hover to incredible high speed at treetop altitudes. At one point, the craft "jumped" over 20 miles in just seconds. Millstadt police officer Craig Stevens had the presence of mind to take a Polaroid picture of the object.

Stephenville Texas UFO

On January 8, 2008 people in Stephenville, Texas reported seeing a large silent UFO that passed by the town, and then came back pursued by fighter jets. Radar data obtained with the Freedom of Information Act showed an uncorrelated target without a transponder that flew across the area and was headed toward George W. Bush's Crawford ranch when it went off radar.

Angels or Aliens

After looking at all the activity of the UFOs over the last 70 years, the question is, "Why are they here?" To me the visitations show a pattern from merely showing themselves in the 1940's and 1950's to penetrating American nuclear bases in the 1970's and 1980's to mass sightings like Belgium, Phoenix, and Illinois in the 80's, 90's and 00's.

So what is their purpose coming here? It seems that initially it was to get us used to their presence. Flying over Washington D.C. on consecutive weekends is a pretty bold statement on their part. It might even be a bit of intimidation as in, hey we are here, and there is nothing you can do about it.

Then the incursions into military bases may have been to examine our military capability or to try to figure out a way to keep us from destroying ourselves. During the time of the military incursions the Cold War between the Soviet Union and the United States was going strong. The UFOs came into nuclear weapons storage areas and even shut down the nuclear missiles. They may be overseeing us in a benevolent way, planning to interfere if it looked like we were headed to World War III. There was even one case where a UFO interfered with a ballistic missile test by flying along with the missile and shooting a beam of light at it causing it to go off course.

Several of our recent Presidents have made some interesting comments on UFOs. President Reagan made a speech at the UN in which he said, "I occasionally think how quickly our differences worldwide would vanish if we were facing an alien threat from outside this world."

George H.W. Bush, who had been the head of the CIA was asked what he knew about UFOs and said, "I know some. I know a fair amount."

Jimmy Kimmel has taken the lead from the docile White House press corps in asking presidents about UFOs. Kimmel asked

Bill Clinton, "If I was president... I'd demand to see all the classified files on the UFOs, because I want to know, I'd want to know what has been going on. DID YOU DO THAT?" Clinton responded, "Sort of."

Kimmel asked Obama the same question, "If I was the president... I would immediately race to wherever they have the files about Area 51 and UFOs, and I'd go through everything to find out what happened." Obama joked, "That's why you will not be president, because that's the first thing that you would do." Then Obama joked again saying, "The aliens won't let it happen. You'd reveal all their secrets, and they exercise strict control over us." Kimmel pressed the issue again, and Obama finally said, "I can't reveal anything."

It seems that all three of presidents know more than they are telling. There was a case where a Japan Airlines 747 was followed by a gigantic UFO for 40 minutes over Alaska. When the FAA investigators met with Reagan's scientific team, the CIA confiscated the radar tapes and other evidence and told the group, "This event never happened. We were never here. And you are all sworn to secrecy."

All of this has made me wonder has our government made a deal with the aliens? I really don't know.

Who are these alien visitors anyway? Are they angels? The Bible talks about the sons of god who were divine beings. Cayce said that the sons of god came to earth to help the souls who had become trapped in matter. Isn't that what UFOs seem to be doing now?

When Jesus ascended into heaven from Mount Olive, two men dressed in white appeared to the people there. Were those men in white the aliens/sons of god? Human civilization has only been around a few million years in a material universe that is 12 billion years old. Can you imagine how many civilizations are out there that are billions of years older than ours?

Edgar Cayce told us that the sons of god were the ones who created Homo sapiens through gene splicing. Are the aliens/sons of god trying to create the fifth root race the same way today? There are certainly many stories of alien abductions that involve alien interest in human reproduction. Of course we are going to be able to change our DNA even without the aliens, but they may be shooting for a more immediate change that we could produce.

The aliens may even be preparing for the earth changes that will occur with the darkening of the sun and the moon. The Bible says that at the time of the end that believers will be "caught up with Jesus in the air." Is this divine intervention or an alien rescue mission or both? George Ritchie, the first person to write about the near death experience in his book, Return from Tomorrow, talked about the possibility of 10,000 space ships coming to earth to help during the end times. Is that possible?

I really think that alien or angels question is very interesting and as time has gone on I have come to believe there may be no difference. Arthur C. Clarke said that "any sufficiently advanced technology is indistinguishable from magic." What are the two beings that we see disappearing and re-appearing like magic? Aliens and angels. The Bible says that Enoch and Melchizedek were not born and did not die, they simple appeared and disappeared. Did they just bean into the world like Star Trek? Or do have both aliens and angels developed so far spiritually that they have the power to move from the world spirit to the world of matter?

Edgar Cayce said that the Alanteans had the power to transpose matter from one end of the universe to the next. If so, they must have been in contact with other civilizations. Cayce talks about UFOs in the following reading:

The entity was among the priestesses of the Mayan experience. It was just before that period when those as from the east had come, and there were the beginnings of the unfoldments of the understanding that there were other portions of the same land, or those that were visiting from other worlds or planets. - 1616-1

Cayce also said that the kind of technology that the aliens have does not come without a spiritual understanding:

Q) Give atomic structure of metal which will prevent the gravitational pull.

(A) It is a long way to these - and there must be determined for what purpose these are to be used before ye may be given how, in what manner. For THESE take hold upon Creative Forces. Show thyself approved, first! - 412-9

THE 2026 AWAKENING

Because of the movement of the Earth with respect to the background stars, every 2,165 years we move from one astrological age to the next. An important event that is occurring during this time period is that we are currently moving from the Age of Pisces to the Age of Aquarius.

One fascinating thing about this is that every time we change from one astrological age to the next, our religious symbols change also. During the previous age, the Age of Aries, the religious symbols revolved around the sign of Aries, a fire sign that is symbolized by the ram. The religious rituals that were used then involved sacrificing rams on an altar of fire. This took place in the Jewish Temple in Jerusalem and is discussed at length in the Old Testament of the Bible. Other religious fire symbols during that time included the menorah, a candle stand in the Temple whose candles were kept burning constantly by attending priests. The Age of Aries ended when the Temple was desecrated by a Syrian king, Antiochus Epiphanes, in 165 B.C.

The present age, the Age of Pisces, has religious symbols that revolve around the sign of Pisces, a water sign symbolized by the fish. Jesus was the physical embodiment of the Piscean Age. He walked on water, calmed the water, was baptized in water, turned water into wine, multiplied the fishes and the loaves, called the fish into the nets, and He was even called the fisher of men. People today even use the Greek word for fish, Ichthus, as a symbol for Jesus. In addition Pisces is the martyr's sign, and the Piscean Age began with the martyrdom of Jesus.

The next age, the Age of Aquarius, will have religious symbols that will revolve around the sign of Aquarius, an air sign symbolized by a man carrying a pitcher of water. So the religious symbols will involve a man pouring out a pitcher of water and the air. Perhaps the religious rituals will involve some type of breathing exercises like yogic breathing. This New Age will begin with the 1,000 years of peace predicted in the Bible and by Cayce. It will be characterized by a world united in universal brotherhood, and it will begin very soon.

How soon? No one can tell for sure, but during the period 2024 to 2027 there are some very rare and powerful astrological aspects. I think that might be the time.

Why do I think this? Because when the big, slow-moving planets like Uranus and Neptune line up in good aspect, it creates opportunities for human culture to advance. These periods only occur every 30 years, so it is a very rare thing. Fortunately for us, this time is coming very soon.

Predicting the Future Using Astrology

Two thousand years ago there were wise men who attended the birth of Jesus. They were called the magi. Who were the magi? The word magi means "one who studies the stars" or astrologers. So the magi were astrologers who knew about the birth of Jesus by studying the stars. Can we predict future events the same way today? I think so.

The movement of the planets in space affect individuals and world events. When negative astrological aspects occur, negative things happen on the earth. When positive astrological aspects occur, we have times of peace and prosperity on the earth. Astrological aspects affect world events. This chapter will explore how the planets influenced events on earth during the past and how they will influence events in the future.

First, let's look at how astrology works. In astrology 60 degree and 120 degree aspects are good, and 90 degree and 180 degree aspects are bad. That is all there is to astrology.

How do we know this? It has been proven by science. When the planets are at 90 and 180 degree aspects, it creates solar storms in the solar system. This is the physical proof of the astrological influences of bad aspects which astrologers call squares and oppositions.

The 60 and 120 degree aspects are called sextiles and trines. They are so important, that the Hebrews arranged to celebrate their holiest day, Yom Kippur, only when the sun and the moon were 120 degree apart. This is called a trine, and it is the most positive of all the astrological aspects. Because the Jewish calendar is a lunar calendar, the sun and the moon are always trine each other on Yom Kippur, the Day of Atonement.

In April of 1941, Edgar Cayce gave several readings in which he said that the astrological aspects at that time were very unusual. In the following, Gertrude Cayce, Edgar Cayce's wife, conducted the reading:

Mrs. Cayce: In the light of the information given through this channel this morning, April 28, 1941, regarding astrological aspects for the next two weeks, and our desire to use this for the good of all, you will please advise us as to the character of changes to take place and how we may constructively meet them. You will then answer the questions, as I ask them.

Mr. Cayce: Yes, we have the information that has been indicated through these channels regarding astrological influences and their effect upon the future thought of each soul now manifesting in the earth.

As is understood by many, in the earth manifestation and the cycle of time much repeats itself; and those in authority, in high and low places, have the opportunity for individual expression—that wields an influence upon those who are directed in body, mind or thought or spirit by the activities of those manifesting in the earth.

As to those experiences paralleling the cycle of astrological activity now—beginning on the morrow—there will be the Sun, the Moon, Jupiter, Uranus and Venus all in the one sign.

When last this occurred, as indicated, the earth throughout was in turmoil, in strife.

There are still influences indicated in the lives of groups banded as nations, banded as peoples, still influenced by those happenings.

What then, ye ask, is the influence that makes for this great change that may be expected?

The powers of light and darkness, as then, as sixteen hundred (1600) years before. As in those periods, so today—we find nation against nation; the powers of death, destruction, the wrecking of that which has been and is held near and dear to the hearts of those who have through one form or another set ideals. 3976-26

From astrological aspects every soul in the earth, in the present experience, will think differently, will have varied urges from the happenings as will come to pass in the next two weeks. Not merely because of the unusual astrological aspects, but more because each entity through its awareness in physical consciousness, in cosmic consciousness, has come in the environ of the ruling forces of the astrological aspects that are to be so active in the affairs of man in his relationships one to another during this period—from April the 29th to May the 12th, 1941. It has been over eight hundred years since such has been the urge. Think of the darkness of the spiritual life as was enacted then, and see what is the experience through which so many souls are passing and will pass during this period in the relationships of man to man. 2550-1

The readings tell us that it had been hundreds of years since the astrological influences were as unusual as they were in the spring of 1941. He said that it was a time when the forces of light and darkness were battling on the earth. These influences can be easily seen by looking at the astrological aspects for May 10, 1941.

The Bombing of London
May 10, 1941

On that day there was a conjunction of the Sun, Mercury, Venus, Jupiter, Saturn, and Uranus in the sign of Taurus. These planets were all in a bad aspect with Mars and the Moon. The arrangement was the familiar T-square, the worst configuration in astrology.

What is interesting about this grouping is that all the planets are square Mars, the planet of war, violence, and aggression: Sun square Mars, Moon square Mars, Mercury square Mars, Jupiter square Mars, Saturn square Mars, and Uranus square Mars. It does not get any worse than this with regard to war and violence.

May 10, 1941, was the date of the worst bombing raid on London during all of World War II. The Germans dropped incendiary bombs, which the winds whipped into a firestorm that destroyed 10,000 buildings and killed thousands of people.

If one looks at what was going on in the world on that day, one could almost say it was the low point for civilization in the 20th century. Stalin was in power in Russia, Tojo in Japan, and Hitler in Germany. The Germans had conquered most of Europe, and England was fighting alone against Hitler. This was all reflected in the astrological aspects of that time and day.

The Berlin Wall falls

On November 9, 1989, the most important event of the last quarter of the 20th century occurred….the fall of the Berlin Wall. When the East Germany government announced that the borders would be opened that day, thousands of Germans appeared at the border demanding to be allowed to cross. The border guards had no choice except to open the gates and the reunification of Germany began. This led ultimately to the fall of the Soviet Union.

The Berlin Wall Falls
November 9, 1989

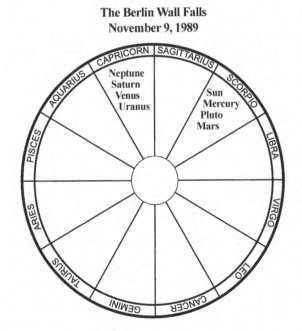

Later that month, on November 29, 1989, a large triangular UFO appeared over the town of Liege in Belgium. Over the next several months this triangular UFO appeared again and again and was witnessed by many thousands of people, sometimes at very close range. It was the most amazing UFO wave in human history.

So I thought, "What were the astrological aspects during that time period, and when will we see those again?"

At that time the Sun, Mercury, Venus, Mars, Saturn, Uranus, Neptune, and Pluto were all lined up in positive aspect. But here is the key point....Saturn, Uranus, and Neptune were all together in Capricorn. Uranus and Neptune move so slowly that they only aspect each other every 30 years or so. Neptune represents spiritual ideals and outer space, and Saturn represents physical manifestation, so this was the perfect aspect for political change and UFO visitation, and we had the greatest political change in decades and the biggest UFO wave ever.

So, when will we see these types of astrological aspects again? Between 2024 and 2027.

2024 to 2027

The astrological aspects from 2024 to 2027 are the best astrological aspects we will see in the first half of the 21st century. This is because Uranus and Neptune move very slowly through the zodiac, and from 2024 to 2027 they will be in good aspect with each other. This is an extremely rare aspect that happens only once every thirty years or so. It represents a great opportunity for the human race to develop its psychic and mystic powers and evolve to a higher level of spiritual understanding. Once again, I cannot emphasis how rare and how good these aspect are. Keep that in mind.

Uranus is the planet of extremes....very, very good and very, very bad. Since it will be mostly in good aspect during this time period, it will be a time of extremely good change. In the mundane world Uranus rules the fields of television, computers, and electronics.

Neptune is the planet of mysteries and mysticism. In positive aspect it gives the dreams and visions that inspire us to do great things. In negative aspect it gives the confusion and delusion that leads us down the wrong path. Positive Neptune aspects provide intuitive understanding of the spiritual mysteries of life. This understanding often comes in the form of powerful and prophetic dreams, since dreams fall within the realm of Neptune's influence.

In mythology, Neptune was the ruler of the sea, and the planet Neptune is the ruler of liquids, large bodies of water, and outer space. In the career world, a prominent Neptune can lead a person to a job in chemistry, the movies, or anything involving the ocean or bodies of water. Neptune, however, is not considered the planet of the practical. It is more for the dreamers, the mystics, and the intuitives.

Uranus with Neptune working together create the possibility for extreme religious and mystical change for the better. This time period could be the fulfillment of the prophecies of the Bible and the Cayce readings and the time of first contact with our alien friends.

The Great Pyramid, the Sphinx, and the Equinoxes

The Cayce readings say that some of the prophecies in the Great Pyramid were correct as to the hour, day, year, place, country, nation, town, and individuals involved. That's how specific the prophecies built into the Great Pyramid and the Sphinx are according to Cayce.

But what time and day? As we saw earlier, the Great Pyramid was built to show its eight sided shadow only during sunrise and sunset on the spring and fall equinoxes. Why? I believe it was to predict an event that will occur on that exact day and at that exact time.

The same thing is true of the Sphinx. The Sphinx lines up perfectly with the sun on the spring equinox and the fall equinox. So the Sphinx gazed to the east for 12,000 years waiting for one particular day.

March 20, 2026

The astrological aspects for the year 2026 are the best aspects we will see in any year in the first half of the 21st century. So could 2026 be the year of the return of Jesus and the opening of the Hall of Records at Giza? I think so.

The position of the sun at sunrise on the spring equinox indicates what astrological age we are in. So the change from the Age of Pisces to the Age of Aquarius will occur on one particular spring equinox at dawn.

The equinox with the best astrological aspects in the next 35 years is the spring equinox, March 20, 2026. These aspects are most powerful at sunrise as the Moon, Venus, Saturn, Neptune, and the Sun all come over the horizon together. This is a spectacular configuration! This group is lined up in good aspect with Uranus and Pluto. It represents the physical manifestation of spiritual ideals.

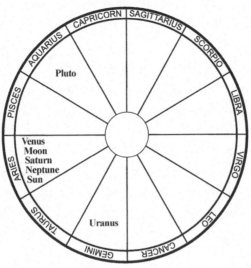

Sunrise Spring Equinox
Cairo, Egypt
March 20, 2026

Edgar Cayce said that planets have their greatest influence, when they are on the ascendant or the midheaven. On that day in 2026, you have the power of the Sun with Neptune the Mystic and Saturn the Builder, directly on the ascendant at sunrise. They are lined up with Uranus the Psychic and Pluto, the planet of regeneration. If you were to design a chart for the return of Jesus and the beginning of the new age, you couldn't design a better one than this.

Also on that day, Jupiter is in good aspect with Mars and Mercury. Jupiter is the ennobling planet, Mars is the masculine planet, and Mercury represents the mind. Combined with the mystical aspects of the Sun, Neptune, Uranus, Saturn, and Pluto, this is an amazing lineup of planets.

This configuration of the Sun, Saturn, Neptune, Uranus, and Pluto is very similar to the configuration we looked at in November of 1989 when the Berlin Wall fell and when the triangle UFOs first appeared over Belgium. This gives you an idea of what kind of amazing events are possible in March of 2026. Powerful political changes combined with alien visitations. That is what we have to look forward to.

Edgar Cayce said that Jesus was born on March 19, 4 B.C. The 2026 spring equinox, March 20th, is almost exactly 2,030 years to the day of Jesus' birth. Is this a coincidence? Perhaps not.

What will be the timeline of events?

By using the predicted events we can arrive at a timeline. The first event predicted is the invasion of the Middle East. The prophets tell us that this invader will be destroyed by fire. After this event, the sun and the moon will be darkened, and Jesus will return to earth. Then there will be the opening of the Hall of Records under the Sphinx, and the thousand years of peace will begin.

As far as the astrology goes, the United States has some very warlike aspects in the early 2020's that come to a head in 2025. Then the best aspects for the world come in 2026 and 2027. Specifically, the spring equinox 2026, August 2026, and the spring equinox 2027, all have great astrological aspects. We will see some amazingly positive changes during the years 2026 and 2027.

What will the Age of Aquarius be like?

There is very little in the prophecies to tell us what the new age will be like. So I went back and looked at the Edgar Cayce readings on Atlantis to get some kind of glimpse at what the future may be like.

Cayce tells us that the continent of Atlantis existed at a very high spiritual and technological level for thousands of years. He says that Atlantis was ruled by a man named Amilius who, according to Cayce, was a previous incarnation of Jesus.

The Atlanteans had a crystal power source and could beam this power from place to place. In addition Cayce says they had the ability to transpose matter from one end of the universe to the next, just like they beam things from place to place on *Star Trek*.

The Atlanteans also had a spiritual understanding that included the use of occult powers such as telepathy, telekinesis, etc. Cayce says that among the Atlanteans such powers were commonplace.

One of the most interesting descriptions of Atlantis in the Cayce readings involves a crystal room. Apparently, the initiates would enter a room with an enormous crystal in the center and go into an altered state of consciousness, that is, go out of the body. Then through this crystal they could communicate with what Cayce called "angelic forces." Could this be our alien friends? Whether it be aliens or angels, I believe both will be a part of our experience once the world reaches this new age.

Five Great Things That Will Happen in the Future

1. The Opening of the Hall of Records
   A repository of ancient knowledge, the Hall of Records, will be opened soon. These records are in three places: underwater off the coast of Bimini, in the Yucatan in Central America, and by the Sphinx in Egypt.

2. A New Type of Human Body
   There will be a new type of human body after Jesus returns. We call this new body the fifth root race. This is not a race like we normally think of race as in black, white, yellow, brown, and red, but a new human race with a new type of physical body.

3. First Contact with the Aliens

   I believe that our first contact with our alien friends will occur during the beginning of the new age. Once humans reject war, they will be accepted by the higher civilizations in the universe.

4. A Thousand Years of Peace on the Earth

   There will be a thousand years of peace on the earth after the new age begins. No more war, no more bloodshed, or oppression will happen anywhere in the world. It will be the greatest time in human history.

5. The Return of Jesus

   The return of Jesus to Earth.

Conclusion

As time goes by, I believe we need to give more and more thought about our own attitude toward the new age. The great tribulation and the changes in the earth are merely the birth pains, something which is unpleasant but which must be experienced if this new world is to be born. We should not look on the changes with fear, even though it is hard not to sometimes.

As Richard Bach wrote in his book *Illusions,* "What the caterpillar calls the end of the world, the master calls a butterfly." It all depends on your point of view when you look at it.

The new age will, I am sure, be totally different than we think it will be. It will be more dynamic and beautiful and will affect more people than we can imagine. The entire world will undergo a tremendous transformation, a revolutionary change on all levels.

When Jesus appears, He will be loving and forgiving. He will embody all the positive characteristics a human being can have. He will be as wonderful as we expect Him to be, and more . . . God's love flowing through one man.

His mere physical appearance is not the extent of the change, however, for He stood in people's presence 2,000 years ago, and it did not change their hard hearts. Thus, the change must be within us, and as such we all have a part in the new age. This is a great opportunity for all of us, for we can be a part of the most joyous change in the history of humankind. No one will be kept from participating if he or she wants to. We need to prepare ourselves mentally and spiritually for this new day, first through the desire to be a part of it and then through actions to make it come about in a more positive fashion. If in our day-to-day living we reflect God's love, we will be contributing positively to the atmosphere of expectancy. If we can be a little kinder, a little more forgiving, we will be contributing to the change. This is surely what is needed in the world today.

In the way of physical preparations, these need to be made, but this has been overemphasized by many people. It is said that we should head for the countryside, build fortresses, store food, and prepare for the end. The term "survivalists" has been coined by the press to describe people who preach this type of preparation. Even though storing food may be a good idea, in general the "survivalist" attitude isn't the best attitude to take. John

White, author of *Pole Shift*, tells a story about a group of survivalists in Oregon. They bought land in the country, built underground bunkers, stored food, brought in their yogurt makers and Browning automatic rifles to prepare themselves for the disintegration of society at the end of the age. A year after the group formed, the leader died of a heart attack. The doctors said it was stress related!

Obviously, he took the wrong attitude toward the coming changes, seeing them as confrontational. Our mental and spiritual preparation is more important than the physical. No amount of physical preparation is going to save you if you are not ready spiritually.

This new age is something to be looked forward to with great joy. Political, economic, and social institutions will be set up on a much more equitable basis than they are today. No wars, strife, civil disorder, oppression, or denial of people's rights will be tolerated.

No more will the nations of the world waste trillions of dollars on weapons of destruction as they do today. Those resources will go to the improvement of life for every individual soul on the earth.

A new brand of science will emerge based on the understanding of the One Force in the universe. This science will extend life expectancy far beyond what it is today. People will live a long, long time, as we are told they did in biblical times. Some may live as long as Methuselah who, according to the Bible, lived to be over 900 years old.

The purpose of this new age will not be just to snatch a few souls up to heaven, leaving the rest behind. Rather, the purpose of the new age is to continue the work of saving souls from separation from God. The greatest sin is to be separated from God or to be unaware of His presence, and a soul can only will this on itself. For as has been said, "God has not willed that any soul should perish but has prepared for each a way of escape." An all knowing, all loving God would not want for any to perish, not *one*. So during the thousand years of peace and after, the work of soul attunement will go on.

All that is necessary for us to be a part of this new world is a desire to be there and the willingness to align our wills with God's will. I hope that everyone who reads this will experience the great joy that lies ahead.